Positive Aging

A SMART Living 365 Guide To

Thriving & Wellbeing At Any Age

Kathy Gottberg

Positive Aging

A SMART Living 365 Guide to
Thriving & Wellbeing at Any Age

Cover Design and Illustration: Thom Gottberg
Cover Models: Kathy Manley Edwards, Kathy Gottberg, Kloe Gottberg & PJ Dondero

ISBN-13: 978-1974614233

ISBN-10: 1974614239

ALSO BY KATHY GOTTBERG

BOOKS

The Findhorn Book of
Practical Spirituality

The Complete Guide to Selling Your Own Home
In California

Finding Grace
A Transformational Journey

Simple * SMART & Happy
A SMART Living 365 To A Sustainable & Meaningful Lifestyle

Rightsizing
A SMART Living 365 Guide to Reinventing Retirement

WEBSITES

SMART Living 365.com

KathyGottberg.com

ACKNOWLEDGEMENTS

Nothing I've ever done or written was completed on my own. I am thankful every day of my life for all who have crossed my path. However, my deepest gratitude is for my husband Thom who is my best friend and muse.

I also owe a debt of gratitude to four "Accountability Partners" who helped me with reading this book and offering feedback. They are Julia Robinson, Karen Vielhaber, Larry Kelly and Mary Lawson. Your generosity of time and talent is highly valued and appreciated. I am also grateful to Joanne Mintz and Lessley Currier for their valuable final proofing.

In addition, I want to thank the hundreds of followers on my blog SMART Living 365.com. It is because of you that I know what information should be included in this book. You told me what you liked and what you found helpful and it is my sincere hope that these words reach out and touch those who can benefit most from a simple change in your mind, heart and lifestyle.

Table of Contents

Introduction

"Getting old is a fascinating thing. The older you get, the older you want to get." ~Keith Richards

Like most people, I never spent much time thinking about aging when I was younger. Even though I hit a few bumps in my forties and fifties, I managed to hold stubbornly to the belief that I was merely middle aged. Like many others, I somehow felt I was an exception to getting older. The idea of being over the hill, or even approaching the hill, just didn't seem to apply to me. Then I turned 60 and I began to feel that things had changed.

It wasn't so much that I suddenly felt old. Fortunately I am quite active and in reasonably good health, and so is my husband Thom. During our 50s, we had gradually begun making choices that helped to secure our financial security by taking steps to "rightsize" * our life. We also took up daily meditation to help with our mental and emotional attitude. In addition, we had slowly improved our diet and increased our physical activities. Yet in spite of how those choices benefited us in many ways, 60 still felt different.

Part of the problem was that I didn't feel old, but the evidence was obvious that I was long past being young. And while I had convinced myself that I fit into middle age for a while, that label also began to feel outdated and inaccurate. That's when I realized that the biggest problem is that my view of aging and the experience of getting older didn't match. It wasn't that I felt bad—but my view of aging carried heavy baggage and needed to be revamped.

Once I started looking around, I noticed an increasing number of people who were 20 to 30 years older than me who radiated vitality and zest for life. Not only were their brains sharp and curious, but the light shining from their eyes proved that age is nothing but a number. Sure I could see a few people who were struggling with difficult conditions and circumstances. Yet at the same time, many elders far older than me appeared to be in splendid condition—emotionally, spiritually, physically and financially. I also began noticing new studies and research being done around the world that showed that aging usually continues to be a very productive and positive phase in the majority of people's lives.

Through it all, I was strongly reminded that we all get to choose what we focus on in any given moment. I don't pretend it is always easy, but I believe it is possible. I routinely do my best to pay attention to my thinking and keep my mind trained on the positive in every area of my life. So it's logical that for me that coming up with positive ways to view aging needed to be the next step in my awareness.

But what do we call it? As I've learned, and you will too in the following chapters, what we think about the aging process matters a great deal. Think you are over-the-hill? Then chances are good that you will gradually experience more and more evidence that proves your point. Think that you are resilient, energetic and constantly growing no matter what your age or circumstances? Then chances are you will adjust and continue to be optimistic about your future no matter what comes along.

That led me to explore different words and labels for this next stage of life. Some people are attempting to redefine the word "old" to help overcome the ageism that is rampant in our culture. But again, if we can't let go of the cultural bias that the word old contains, we might be losing the battle. Others call it the "third-act" meaning we have passed youth, middle age, and now find ourselves at a new stage. But that term sounds too vague to me to transform my thinking about the ongoing process.

At one point I joined what I thought was an older women's wisdom group to see if that fit. Unfortunately when they began calling themselves "crones", it just didn't work for me. While that archaic word might carry some positive attributes, our society continues to hold a negative belief about the perception. Elderly or senior doesn't feel right either.

In case you are wondering, I don't yet have a replacement title for the aging progression. But perhaps that is just as it should be. Because many of us are experiencing a vastly different experience of what it means to be over 60, 70 or 80, it makes sense that we haven't yet uncovered what positive aging means in this day and age. But one thing I know for sure, the more of us who reach these ages with a positive and optimistic perspective, the more we are changing everything it means to age in our world.

Does this book only help those of us 60 and older? No! I sincerely wish that someone had given me a book like this when I was in my 40s or 50s The more we keep reminding each other that we have much to look forward to in the future, the better. The more we tell those younger than us that aging can be wonderful, the better. Instead of worrying about what is coming as we age, holding a positive perspective is sure to keep our minds open to our options. And as the saying goes, like fine wine, we just get better with age.

To help us along, this book is filled with the best ideas about aging that I have discovered in the last couple of years and posted on my blog. There should be no surprise that it comes from the most positive standpoint I can find. I continue to believe that it is wise and encouraging to do our best to reach for the most optimal viewpoint for the future, no matter what circumstances come along in our individual lives. And of course, like my other books from my blog, my thoughts are my own and many of the examples come from my life. I'm not a trained professional by any means. Instead I am a person like you who wants to continue to live a happy, healthy and meaningful life as long as possible.

We are all in different places on the journey of life but we do share many of the same challenges and rewards. By learning from one another and staying open to the good and possible, the next 30+ years can be as good, or better than the last. Join me as I explore what it means to age in a SMART** and positive way.

* Rightsizing is the word I use to describe the process of focusing on what is best for you individually as you age and move toward retirement. My book, **Rightsizing For Retirement** is available on Amazon as both an ebook and in print.

** Just about every article I write on my blog SMART Living 365.com comes from a perspective I believe to be SMART. Whenever I use the word SMART (all caps) it points to that idea.

Chapter 1

Why I Don't Think I'm Old And Don't Think You Should Think It Either

I've always said that I will never let an old person into my body. That is, I don't believe in 'thinking' old. Don't program yourself to break down as you age with thoughts that decline is inevitable. ~Wayne Dyer

I arrived on this planet 62 years ago, and I don't think I'm old. Sure, I've been around a while and have certainly aged. But again, I don't think that necessarily makes me old. Then this last week a friend and fellow blogger wrote an article saying that it was "ageist" to deny that we aren't old past a certain age. While my friend didn't mention when that exact number occurs, just knowing she is only a year or two older than me, made me guess that she believes I'm in the same boat. But the thing is, I don't think she is old either, regardless of her age.

Of course, I do agree with her that rampant age discrimination exists in our country. It's been around for as long as I can remember and I'm guilty of it too. I distinctly recall thinking my parents were old when I introduced Thom to them back in the late 1970s. At the time, they were in their early 40's, and I am now two decades older than them at that introduction. Your perspective clearly changes as you age and until you reach certain milestones yourself, it is tough to relate.

At the same time, I am not the same age as my mother was when she was 62. Even if we compare the same calendar years, her attitude, her health, her enthusiasm (or lack thereof), her relationships and her outlook on life all put her in a dramatically different reality. Demanding that all of us claim that we are old past a certain age, without considering significant life characteristics and conditions doesn't work for me. Haven't we all met people who are "old" in their 30s?

But make no mistake; I'm not into denying my age whatsoever. I freely tell people the number if they ask, but don't let their definition of that define me. I agree that my body doesn't look the same as it used to, or that I have all the same physical attributes that I possessed at certain phases of my life. Sure, I've had some health issues and am battered and bruised a bit. However, rather than focus on what I have lost, I spend far more time thinking about what I've gained instead.

- My health is good, and I'm able to do everything I want to do physically at this point in my life.
- My marriage has deepened and grown tremendously through the years, and I can easily say I am more in love with my husband than I ever even guessed at 40 years ago.
- Our finances are comfortable and secure. The freedom and peace of mind from rightsizing our life is highly rewarding.
- I have the privilege of being a writer and can express my creativity and myself on a regular basis.
- I feel my writing and my other actions are a service to the world providing me with meaning and purpose.
- I love and accept myself to a significant degree.

I realize that not everyone who is 62 can claim these blessings. But should I deny all the good in my life to make others feel better? Or is it necessary to throw us all under the same bus just because they don't apply to everyone?

Another reason I count myself fortunate is that I have a couple of great role models who live and work nearby who have aged in extremely positive ways. My hometown is near Palm Springs, CA in a desert community long considered a retirement haven in

Southern California. One of my friends, a successful restaurateur is opening his second local restaurant this fall. He just turned 80 and wears me out trying to keep up with all he and his wife have going on in their lives.

Other friends are a couple, aged 93 and 92, who stay active in business, philanthropy, and life. I have never once heard them call themselves old and I surely don't think of them that way. They demonstrate repeatedly that an advanced age does not make you old.

Of course, like I said earlier, I do believe that ageism is a problem in our culture. Open any magazine and the majority of people you see are young and predominantly Anglo. That is until you come to an article about health, certain pharmaceuticals, and/or insurance and they nearly always depict aged people with gray hair and wrinkles. The implication is that older people should focus on health and security, while younger people get to have all the fun. Rewriting that theme from old age to positive aging is critically needed in my opinion.

The way I see it, we all have two ways to address the ageism prejudice. First, we can require everyone to redefine "old" from the commonly accepted word in use for millennia. Part of that requirement would ask that everyone over the age of 50 or beyond to start calling themselves "old," 24/7. And regardless of how you feel, what you do, and the circumstances of your life, you just accept that old is what you are.

The second way to address the issue is to start promoting the idea of positive aging. Positive aging does not deny that aging carries certain liabilities. It does not endorse the idea that we go from middle age to death without any experience in between. It does not recommend that we act, dress, talk and live as though we are younger than we are. Instead, it fully embraces the good along with the less than desirable of who we are in the present moment, while still staying actively engaged with life as much as possible.

And it matters. As you'll read in the following pages, what we think about aging affects us on a mental, emotional and physical manner. Besides impacting our attitude in all sorts of positive ways, a study performed at Yale University by Becca Levy and others reports that people who view aging in a positive way live on average an extra seven and a half years. Yes! You add seven and a half years to your life by holding on to the self-perception that aging is a positive experience rather than a negative one. Which do you choose?

I get it. I know that not everyone is as healthy as they would like to be. When our bodies don't perform the way they did when we were younger, we tend to compare them in ways that are usually less than positive. But if we neglect

19

to address all the beneficial aspects of aging, we make our existence totally reliant on the condition of our bodies. I happen to believe that our true selves are so much more than just that alone.

Perhaps rather than trying to convince ourselves that it is okay to be old, we should instead spend time focusing on what it means to be vibrantly alive at any age. I don't think that's ageist, I think that's SMART. Enthusiasm, curiosity, love of learning, eagerness, excitement and positively anticipating the future all add up to a person who is not only aging well, but someone who will likely be alive seven and a half years later. And while all of us are certainly growing older every single day, I think the SMART choice is to refuse to call yourself old. Instead, I'm going to start calling myself and others I admire, "well-aged."

Chapter 2

Ten Awesome Benefits to Growing Older

Your 40s are good. Your 50s are great. Your 60s are fab. And 70 is f*@king awesome! ~Helen Mirren

Just about every day I read a post on Facebook or one of the many blogs I follow about getting older. And while many of them poke fun at the experience, most of the time the articles subtly (or not so subtly!) talk about the drawbacks to aging. But, when you think about it, every single day each of us is getting older—and thankfully so! Consider the alternative. So instead of thinking of life as a gradual decline, let's all start thinking of how life gets better as we go along—and that the advantages far outweigh the disadvantages. Perhaps a good way to prepare is to start focusing on those benefits today.

Here are ten great benefits we gain as we age:

1) **Less negativity—higher self esteem.** Researcher Ulrich Orth from the University of Basel studied thousands of 18

to 89 year olds and discovered that regardless of demographic and social status, the older we get the more negativity diminishes and the higher our self-esteem climbs. He says, "With time, we hone qualities like self-control and altruism that contribute to overall happiness. The best is yet to come!" A large Gallup Poll done in 2008 confirmed that adults near 85 years old are even more satisfied with themselves and their life than they were at 18.

2) **More positive wellbeing—greater emotional stability.** Laura Carstensen, a professor of psychology at Stanford University recently published a study where she showed that as time passed over a 15 year period her study subjects reported more positive well-being and greater emotional stability as they aged—no matter what their age when they started the study. Carstensen's studies show that negative emotions like sadness, anger and fear become less pronounced as we age as opposed to the roller-coaster drama-filled younger years. Even further, the Gallup Poll done in 2008 reported that stress and worry gradually decline from teenage years and reach a low point when a person turns 85 years old.

3) **Brain plasticity.** It was once believed that we were born with a certain number of brain cells that slowly died off as we age. Science now knows that our brains continue to grow neurons as we age and can reshape itself in response to what it learns. Even learning to juggle, learning a new language or playing an instrument can cause significant brain changes in hearing, memory and hand movements. Plus, studies confirm that our vocabulary not only continues to grow as we do, it becomes richer and provides more subtle ways of expressing ourselves. As long as we use it, we won't lose it!

4) **Synced hemispheres.** Brain scans show that while young people often use only one side of their brain for a specific task, middle age and older adults are more likely to activate both hemispheres at the same time—a pattern known as bilateralization. This process allows more mature people to use the full power of their brain when faced with problems or situations. Specifically, our reasoning and problem-solving skills tend to get sharper.

5) **Clearer priorities.** Studies done by Michael Marsiske Ph.D. suggest that older adults tend to perceive time in a way that makes them

"increasingly aware that our years on this Earth are limited." He goes on to say that, "This awareness helps explain the choices that older adults tend to make: to spend time with a smaller, tighter circle of friends and family, to pay more attention to good news than to bad news, and to seek out positive encounters and avoid negative ones." In other words, aging helps us let go of the trivial and focus on what is most important.

6) **Wiser perspective.** A study done at the University of Michigan presented "Dear Abby" letters to 200 people and asked them what advice they would give. Those over 60, as opposed to younger participants, offered a wider variety of options showing different points of view, multiple resolutions and suggested compromise. One theory is that as we age we develop a multitude of brain maps that help us to recognize and respond to similar circumstances when we come upon them again. By midlife and beyond we have a stockpile of these maps, which offer us a sense of effortless mastery from our wealth of experiences.

7) **Better Able To See Big Picture.** Allison Sekuler, PhD. did a study in 2005 where younger and older subjects were shown

moving objects on a computer screen of varying shapes and shades. While younger people were able to point them out more quickly when they were small and gray, older subjects had the advantage when they were large and highly contrast. Sekuler noted that young brains seemed better able at focusing on details to the exclusion of their surroundings while more mature brains can take in the entire scene. Need some big picture thinking—ask a senior!

8) **See the good—ignore the bad.** As we age our brains gradually begin reacting less to negative input and are pulled more toward the positive. Laura Carstensen director of the Stanford Center on Longevity did a study in 2004 where younger and older volunteers were asked to observe happy, distressed and neutral photographs. The brains of younger subjects (18-29) were activated equally by happy or distressed images. Meanwhile, the brains of the older subjects (70-90) reacted much more strongly to the positive photos. Then later when asked to recall some of the photos, the older group conveniently were unable to remember having seen the distressing photos as opposed to the younger group.

9) **Higher Work Satisfaction.** A recent study by the Associated Press & NORC Center For Public Affairs found that 92% of workers aged 50 or older say they are very or somewhat satisfied with their job, while only 80% of those under 30 report the same thing. Only 38% of young adults say they are deeply satisfied with their work, while 63% of those age 65 and older admit to such deep satisfaction. It is believed that by the time we age to a certain level we have found the type of work that we feel is fulfilling and satisfying.

10) **Self-Appreciation And Acceptance.** While this benefit is not a given for everyone who ages, those who age successfully and with contentment embrace the need for self-love. After a certain age the futility of trying to be someone else or to make others happy to our detriment becomes pointless, and the freedom and courage to be oneself becomes paramount. Often this means recognizing that our true value and worth has little to do with how we look or what we do in the world, and everything to do with who we really are on a soul level.

Sure there are some downsides to the aging process, but I'm convinced it is time to start focusing on the upside instead. Face it, when we point out the negatives without the benefits, we tell ourselves and those younger than us that the best part of life is over once we hit a certain age. And frankly, my experiences so far don't even come close to that being true.

Now at over 60, my life is at a wonderful place physically, mentally and emotionally. And even if I must gradually give in some on the physical side, the benefits on the mental and emotional side of the equation more than offset the trade. After all, the only way our culture will ever turn the tide to recognizing, honoring and valuing the experience of age is if we fearlessly face it ourselves. I think it's SMART to be ready—what about you?

*Reference to the individual studies quoted in this article are available through links found on SMARTLiving365.com.

Chapter 3

Avoiding Regrets = A Happier Life

Enjoy the good times and walk away from the bumps.
Even failures can turn positive it you keep going. ~*Carl*
Reiner

A musician friend named Rudi Harst wrote a song titled, **"Shoulda, Coulda, Woulda."** It contains a great reminder that feelings of regret can hold us back from living a happy and fulfilled life. But I suspect that one reason why the song makes us laugh and wince at the same time is because we all wish on some level that we could do one or two things differently, that we'd made at least one *other* choice along the line, or that we've neglected to do something we wished we had.

Still, what I've discovered over the last couple of days is that regret isn't one of those negative emotions like fear, shame or jealousy that has little or no redeeming value. Instead regret can serve as a signpost for pointing out choices and changes that can help us lead a SMART and happier life—365.

Interestingly enough, regret is a little tricky to define precisely because it isn't just an emotion. While regret elicits an emotion, it usually comes along with a judgment or appraisal of something—in other words a choice. In countries like the U.S. where we have a great deal of personal freedom in education, work, and relationships, those choices can lead to feelings of regret. In countries where choice and options are limited, far fewer feelings of regret are reported.

More interesting facts about regret comes from Happify.com which claims that 90% of people (in the U.S. at least) admit to a major regret about something in their lives. Regrets can also vary at different ages, and whether you are a man or a woman. For example 44% of women have romantic regrets while only 19% of men share that feeling.

Other facts suggest that regret is most detrimental to seniors and can lead to depression and illness. A big part of that is because many elders believe it is too late to change. Fortunately, younger adults usually feel they have plenty of time to avoid and alter many of their regrets.

Another fascinating tidbit about regret is that it can occur both because of something a person did, or because of something a person didn't do—in other words, either from our actions or our inactions. According to Thomas Giloviqh and Victoria Husted Medvec from Cornell University, "Actions produce greater regret in the short term; inactions generate more regret in the long run." Beyond that Giloviqh and Medec report, "The most common regret of action was to "[rush] in too soon." But, "When people look back on their lives, it is the things they have *not* done that generate the greatest regret." In fact, over the long-term, inaction is usually regretted 75% more than regrettable action.

But there is good news. **Harvard Healthy Publications** explains that regret can be useful no matter what our age when faced directly. The four main benefits of regret are:

1. Allows us to make sense of our past experiences;

2. Allows us to avoid more or similar mistakes made by others or ourselves;

3. Helps us fix our missteps and guides us toward greater fulfillment.

4. Helps us improve our relationships with others.

Because we can learn from regrets, it is extremely beneficial to recognize our own blunders and those of others. The book, *30 Life Lessons For Living* by Karl

Pillemer, Ph.D. offers five suggestions that can help us avoid such regrets. Pillemer interviewed 1,200 senior Americans, average age 78, and they offered the following advice:

- **Always be honest.** Being honest, trustworthy and "fair and square." According to Pillemer his "experts" unanimously and vehemently agreed that living otherwise leads to certain and eventual regret.

- **Say yes to opportunities.** As mentioned above, most regret comes from inaction rather than our actions. As the quote goes, "Twenty years from now you will be more disappointed by the things you didn't do than by the ones you did do. So throw off the bowlines. Sail away from the safe harbor. Catch the trade winds in your sails. Explore. Dream. Discover."

- **Travel more.** You know I loved this one! What's amazing is that most of the "experts" interviewed in the book admitted that they lived rather small and local lives, yet a part of them deeply regretted not experiencing new places, new people, or new ideas. As Pillemer says, "Don't put off until tomorrow what you can do today."

- **Choose a mate with extreme care.** It's likely that the most important "choice" we make in our lives is the person we marry. Unfortunately, according to the "experts" we usually make three big mistakes when it comes to our life partners. 1) We think love and lust are the same thing; 2) we commit out of desperation; 3) we commit without thinking much at all. Any one of the three can lead to regret.

- **Say it now.** According to Pillemer, "…when it comes to deep, long-lasting regret, the experts pointed instead toward things left unsaid." Their advice? "If you have something to say to someone, do it before it's too late."

Another set of "experts" comes from palliative care nurse and author Bonnie Ware in her book, *The Top Five Regrets of The Dying*. They are:

1. *I wish I'd had the courage to live a life true to myself, not the life others expected of me.* "Most people had not honored even a half of their dreams and had to die knowing that it was due to choices they had made, or not made."

2. *I wish I hadn't worked so hard.* "All of the men I nursed deeply regretted spending so much of their lives on the treadmill of a work existence."

3. *I wish I'd had the courage to express my feelings.* "They settled for a mediocre existence and never became who they were truly capable of becoming."

4. *I wish I had stayed in touch with my friends.* "Everyone misses their friends when they are dying."

5. *I wish I had let myself be happier.* "Many did not realize until the end that happiness is a choice."

According to Happify.com a few current regrets are:

- The biggest regret of all is taking a dissatisfying job just for the money;

- 25% of homeowners have buyer's remorse.

- 29% of adults under 35 believe they have posted something on social media that could harm their career.

- 25% regret sharing selfies.

- 31% regret their tattoos.

Regret doesn't have to be something we deny or pretend never happens to us. Instead, regret can be a wake-up call where we realize we've made a decision (or two) that is leading us away from the peace and happiness we crave. In fact, if we are still alive and able to read this, we can start *right now* following the expert advice that I've shared above. Letting go of our regrets might not be easy, but the SMART thing to do is to allow that action to redirect our lives toward greater happiness, purpose and peace. What are we waiting for?

Chapter 4

Carl Jung And The Art Of Aging Well

For the unlearned, old age is winter; for the learned, it is the season of the harvest. ~Hasidic saying

The late afternoon has always been my favorite time of day. So this weekend when I found a quote by Carl Jung, the Swiss psychiatrist and founder of Analytical Psychology, it grabbed my attention. He said, "The afternoon of life is just as full of meaning as the morning; only its meaning and purpose are different....".

Intrigued I continued to read how Jung believed that the approximate time between ages 56 and 83 offer each of us the opportunity to make the process of aging a positive and life-enhancing experience. Regardless of whether we find ourselves only approaching that "afternoon" of life, or deep within it, the SMART perspective is to learn and stay conscious about what we can do to live an ongoing life of quality and purpose.

Dr. Carl Jung was known for seeing the mystical, metaphorical, archetypical and cyclical aspects of life and then teaching, writing and using them in practical and relevant ways for a meaningful experience. So it's no accident that as he aged he explored what that meant from those various viewpoints. Another quote that sums up his introspection states, "A human being would certainly not grow to be 70 or 80 years old if this longevity had no meaning for the species to which he belongs. The afternoon of human life must also have a significance of its own and cannot be merely a pitiful appendage to life's morning." So for Jung, the aging process was not one of inescapable decline of body, mind and relevancy, but instead a time of progressive refinement of what is essential.

Helping to expand that understanding was Jung's ongoing focus on self awareness, individuation and wholeness. Jung said, "An ever-deepening self-awareness seems to me as probably essential for the continuation of a truly meaningful life in any age, no matter how uncomfortable this self-knowledge may be. Nothing is more ridiculous or unsuitable as older people who act as if they were still young — they lose even their dignity, the only privilege of age. The watch must be the introspection. Everything is revealed in self-knowledge, what is it, what is it intended to, and about what and for what one lives. The wholeness of ourselves is certainly a rationale...". In other words, as we grow older we are all offered the opportunity to find meaning and purpose in becoming whole and wise. Perhaps instead of aging we could call it, "sage-ing."

This sounds logical, but unfortunately what we all too often witness in our culture is an obsession with youth, activity and productivity for as long as a person lives. That's why it is important to note that aging successfully is not always the same as aging consciously or well. Most of the time when talking about aging in Western cultures there is the implication that the "best" way to age is to do everything we can to continue doing what we've always done for as long as possible—and to look equally young while doing it!

Author Lars Tornstam, in his book *Gerotranscendence* emphasizes the problem with that by saying, "…we sometimes erroneously project midlife values, activity patterns and expectations onto old age, and then define these values, patterns and expectations as successful aging. Maybe our projections are not just rooted in midlife, but also in western culture and white middle-class hopes for 'success' to continue into old age." When you think about it, what makes us think that we will be the same person with the same desires at 80 as we are at 50? And why would we want to be the same?

Like Jung, Tornstam instead believes that aging offers us the opportunity to redefine our self and relationships in order to arrive at a new understanding regarding fundamental existential questions about life. This possible natural progression towards maturation and wisdom is a stage he calls "Gerotranscendence." Tornstam explains that those who achieve this state often become, "...less self-occupied and at the same time more selective in the choice of social and other activities." This time of life can offer us, "... an increased feeling of affinity with past generations and a decrease in superfluous social interaction." When a person strives for "gerotranscendence" he or she will likely be less interested in material things and crave "solitary meditation." And like Jung and his striving toward wholeness, Tornstam says, "There is also often a feeling of cosmic communion with the spirit of the universe and a redefinition of time, space, life and death."

But what happens if a person doesn't reach for wisdom, wholeness or gerotranscendence in elder years? Unfortunately, for those unable to respond to this new call for inner growth there is a tendency to experience depression, despair, fear of death and regret. Yet our western culture ignores that and continues to spread the idea that aging is best either denied or concealed, making it obvious that the biggest denial of all is the inevitability of death. And in spite of the goal of us all to hopefully avoid disease, disability, waning mental and physical functioning along with some disengagement with life, there will likely come a time when some, if not all, of those aspects become a part of our experience.

Ultimately it will come down to us answering these questions for ourselves: Does our continued existence at our increasing older age have value? Do we have something to contribute beyond just existing in a fairly well-preserved body and mind, with enough resources to keep us reasonably happy, until it's over? Will we as elders have a purpose that can benefit the world and others, no matter how fit, able and active we are?

Jung addresses these questions by saying, "For the most part our old people try to compete with the young." He further illustrates the denial of older people to take on the role of wise elders by pointing out that most men instead strive to be a brother to their sons, while mothers hope to be the older sister to their daughters.

Rather than step eagerly into a stage of life where we dive deep into self-discovery and then mentor from wisdom, most of us hold on as tightly as possible to what we used to be, and continue thinking the way we used to think. Instead of glorifying the roles we played in the "morning" of our lives, Jung recommends that we let go of what we were and optimistically welcome where we are and where we are going. He said, "…an old man who cannot bid farewell to life appears as feeble and sickly as a young man who is unable to embrace it. And as a matter of fact, it is in many cases a question of the selfsame childish greediness, the same fear, the same defiance and willfulness, in the one as in the other."

One reason I've always enjoyed late afternoon is the beauty I see in the spreading shadows at that time of day. There is also a sense of fulfillment of the day's activities and the chance of reconnection with friends and family over food and camaraderie. Clearly different from the ever-increasing light of the morning or the bright midday sun, late afternoon offers us time to pause, reflect and be thankful before night falls. Maybe that is what Jung understood when he urged us to use the later part of our lives to become more whole by discovering who we are and wisely sharing it with others. And perhaps it is SMART for all of us at any age who want to age well to remember, as Carl Jung said, "The privilege of a lifetime is to become who you truly are."

Chapter 5

Training Your Brain For A Long, Healthy & SMART Life

Anyone who stops learning is old, whether at twenty or eighty. Anyone who keeps learning stays young. The greatest thing in life is to keep your mind young. ~Henry Ford

In case you haven't noticed, I am fascinated by the brain and write about it frequently. That might be because I'm a woman in my early sixties, had a mother diagnosed with Alzheimer's in her early 70's, and have a sister just a couple of years older than me that constantly affirms, "I can't remember anything!" and then does her best to prove it. So, for several reasons including the fact that I'm a writer, I've grown attached to my brain and it's creativity and strive to discover everything I can to help it stay healthy and functioning. As it turns out, we can do plenty. But we have to be willing to take care of and exercise our brains just like we do our bodies, or we'll likely get whatever chance throws our way.

I never thought too much about it when I was younger. Chances are good if you are under 40 you haven't either. But there is an abundance of evidence that proves what you do consistently (even when you are young) will make a difference when you do get older—and guess what? You will get older (consider the alternative!). A research psychologist named Mark Rosenzweig did some of the most well-known and documented studies that prove the neuroplasticity of the brain. He verified that the brain continues to develop anatomically throughout life and can reshape and repair itself based on life experiences.

The majority of Rosenzweig's results were studies done on rats. He and his followers showed that rats placed in cages with toys, ladders, tunnels, running wheels and other varied and unique environments had brains that fared far better than the average "caged" rat. Specifically, the brains of the "stimulated" rats contained larger amounts of a chemical called acetylcholine that is essential for learning. Plus, the playful rats had a cerebral cortex that was 5% heavier and brain volume that was 25% bigger. Beyond rats, it's now been shown that the more education (learning of all types) a person has, the larger number of branches in neurons. All of these indicators show that many people with learning disabilities or other more problematic brain disorders can often change and be rewired to function at a much higher capacity. It also shows that the rest of us, who just want to improve or preserve the functionality of our brains, can do so.

Two of the most dramatic examples of this are presented in the book *The Brain that Changes Itself*, by Norman Doidge, M.D. The first comes from a neuroscientist named Paul Bach-y-Rita, whose father suffered a major stroke at 65. Paul's brother George began working with his father daily, long after traditional stroke rehabilitation usually occurs. George asked his dad to spend hours every day for a year turning normal life experiences into exercises. Within one year, the father went from not being able to walk, speak or go to the bathroom by himself—to returning to work as a teacher at a local community college. It took strong concentrated effort and long hours, but he was able to return to almost normal functioning. The most amazing thing was that after he died nearly 10 years later, they did an autopsy and revealed that the initial stroke had been massive, and until that time, considered completely incapacitating.

Another example in the book is a woman named Barbara Arrowsmith Young who was born in the early 1950s and was considered both physically and mentally retarded. Although blessed with a brilliant memory and a couple of other talents, it was only with highly concentrated effort and her mother's help, that she was able to finish high school, college and then graduate school as well. Eventually she explored the details of her own learning disability. Encouraged by others doing work on the brain, she began drilling and exercising her brain in the areas where she was most challenged. She found that when she spent countless hours perfecting her "weak" brain functions in one area, most of the other weak areas improved as well. She currently has completely recovered from all of her former learning dysfunctions, and now runs a world-famous school with programs for other children and adults that struggle with similar issues as well as autism. Young's story of transformation is inspiration for anyone who needs encouragement for their life—and especially those with exceptional brain challenges.

Doidge's book contains a handful of other equally inspiring stories of brain transformation. But none of the recoveries were quick and easy. In fact, just as no one becomes an athlete by working out for a week or two, no one becomes an expert at anything by taking a weekend course. All the brain rewiring and relearning took hours of concentrated effort. Just like Malcolm Gladwell's "10,000-Hour-Rule" explained in his book, *Outliers,* it takes about 10,000 hours to become a success or be an expert at anything. Changing the very fabric of your brain is possible, but not without effort.

A problem of course is that many adults stop learning anything new after a certain age. Think about it. Pew Research says that nearly 25 % of adults never read a full length book during the last year. My guess is that even fewer actually did and if they did, it was purely for entertainment. In fact, in today's technology-driven lifestyle, large numbers of people don't read anything except a tweet or sound bite here or there. Not only do people look to TV or the internet for their information, they watch the same news station, the same programs, vote the same political party, talk to the same people, and just reprocess the same info day after day after day. Just like rats in an "average" cage, their brains deteriorate and they age quickly.

It's been said that humans think about 50,000 to 65,000 thoughts per day. Unfortunately, about 95% are the same thoughts we had yesterday and the day before. Even though the brain is an amazing biological wonder that even the largest and most expensive computer cannot replicate, many use it in the most dull, routine and uninspired manner possible. It's like having a Lamborghini and driving it only in first gear. In most ways, the term couch potato can apply to both our bodies and our brains. If we continue to allow our brains, just like our bodies, to be vegetables, we should not be surprised when we can't seem to do or think of anything else.

Two highlights of SMART Living are practicing sustainability and responsibility. Both of those remind us to maintain and use what we have for as long as we inhabit this world—and yeah, that includes your brain. In future articles on my blog you can be sure that I will offer more ways to continue the practice. I don't know about you, but I intend to keep my brain busy, happy and "exercised" from here on out!

Chapter 6

10 Reasons Why We Need To Disrupt Aging And Retirement

I don't believe in aging. I believe in forever altering one's aspect to the sun. ~Virginia Woolf

Yesterday I finished reading a new book by Jo Ann Jenkins, the CEO of AARP, called ***Disrupt Aging—A Bold New Path To Living Your Best Life At Any Age.*** Not only did it remind me that the prejudice of ageism is alive and well in our country, it suggests that the way we think about aging and retirement is due for a big shift. While I didn't find the ideas in it as bold as advertised, it did get me thinking about aging and retirement in a few new ways. I was also reminded that the only way such a disruption can ever occur is when enough of us begin to see, think and talk about new and positive ways we can all approach aging in the days to come.

One thing is for sure—humans are incredibly adaptable. And once we grow accustomed to something, it seems like it has been that way forever. Aging and retirement are like that. Even though most of us know we are aging much differently from our grandparents and parents, we tend to forget their experience and the world they lived in was very different. While a long leisurely retirement seems like a given for many baby boomers, a large portion of our grandparents were lucky if they were able to stop working before they died.

Let us not forget that regular monthly Social Security payments didn't exist until 1940 with an official "retirement age" of 65. Based upon the average life expectancy at the time of 58 years, only those fortunate to still be alive would ever claim the benefits. With such a discrepancy between life expectancy and age of benefit, only a small portion of the population ever reaped much of the benefits. After all, the original purpose was to provide a safety net for elderly people without the financial means to live life without working.

Fast-forward a mere 20 years. By 1960 life expectancy jumped to nearly 70 years old. Suddenly most people could imagine a time when they would be able to stop working and generating income to live on for the remainder of their lives. Helping people as they aged even further, in 1966 those 65 and older became eligible for Medicare. So when you think about it, only within the last 50 to 60 years has the idea of certain level of financial security, leisure-time, along with healthcare security become a given. And now, as a 62-year-old female, I have a "life expectancy" model of 20 or more years in which I will be potentially able to draw both Social Security and Medicare Benefits.

Like most baby boomers, I am aware that some of that money that I paid into Social Security and Medicare was paid for from my income. But truth be told, if I live to 85 (as is projected) or even longer which is entirely possible, I will draw out more than I put into the fund. Most of us don't like to think that way because, as I said before, we have grown accustomed to thinking it is something we not only deserve but are entitled to collect, while we live out the remainder of our lives.

Before any of you attempt to defend your right to that money, please know that the book doesn't address that issue whatsoever. Taking a much more politically correct view, along with a position that represents millions of AARP members, Jenkins tiptoes around most controversial questions. Yet, the biggest issue she presents is even though so much has changed through the years, society continues to view aging in an outdated way. In other words, our world has changed but our thinking about aging and retirement is light-years behind the time.

A few out-dated ways of thinking about aging

1. We tend to collectively believe that aging is a huge societal problem and older people are seen as a burden or mostly a problem that needs to be fixed.

2. We often ignore our share of responsibility for certain parts of aging like taking good care of our health and our finances—the choices, options, and abilities are not equal for everyone. Depending upon our sex, our race, our education, and our socio-economics, we either have advantages or disadvantages that should be considered.

3. The best we can hope for as we age is a life of ease, comfort, reasonably good health (and a little entertainment) while we wait out the remainder of our lives.

4. Getting older is all about increasing decline and dependency.

5. We frequently think we must do everything we can to be young, or at least seen as young because only the young have something valuable to offer the world.

6. We tend to blame most of our age-related limitations on getting older when many of those

limitations actually come from an environment and culture that was designed to encourage and support the young.

7. Seniors who work are taking jobs away from young people and adding nothing to the economy.

8. Rather than see all of life as a continuous process of growth and development, many of us consider aging as either having "arrived" or over the hill.

9. We stop celebrating the achievements and milestones of a growing and evolving human once we retire as though nothing worthwhile is occurring.

10. Once we retire or consider ourselves a senior, we often stop planning who we want to become in the days ahead—Jenkins calls that "mindless aging."

If we think about it, most of us can probably come up with more ways that our thinking about aging can and should be disrupted. It is becoming easier to see the discrimination in the media about such issues, but most of that is just reflecting common beliefs within our culture. And let's face it—most of us are guilty as well. Any time we make fun of an older person's capacities, anytime we buy a birthday card insinuating that a person is "over the hill" at a certain age, anytime we focus on the contributions of the young at the expense of the older and wiser, we add to the problem.

What can we do? Jenkins' book offers three areas where disruption is most needed. They are in the areas of health, wealth, and self. Jenkins covers each of these in detail:

Health: Jenkins says, " First, we need to begin to focus on physical and mental fitness instead of diminishment, on preventing disease and improving well-being instead of just treating ailments." She also suggests that we become partners in our own healthcare, instead of passive patients. A huge key to our ongoing fitness and well-being is dependable access to good healthcare for all.

Wealth: According to Jenkins, "We also need to understand that wealth doesn't mean becoming rich beyond your wildest dreams. It does mean having financial resilience to not outlive your money." Jenkins promotes the idea that because so many seniors will want to and need to continue to work by necessity, that an "active, employed older population has the potential to be more of an economic boom than a social challenge." She firmly believes that older people will be key drivers of economic growth, innovation and new value creation in the future.

<u>Self:</u> As Jenkins states, " ...we must change the way we view ourselves and our inner lives from aging as decline, to aging as continuous growth." Instead of diminishing, Jenkins suggests that we "develop a sense of purpose and positive self-image" in ways that will increase our confidence and keep us actively engaged in all that life offers.

Of course, those three issues are also tied to a few other ideas like the importance of where and how we want to live in the future. Ninety percent of all adults say they want to "age in place" but either ignore the reality of their current home and community or insist on remaining in locations that are not supportive of advancing physical limitation. But think about it, many homes today were built to reflect a time when life expectancy was less than fifty. Rather than update our thinking and designs, we blame an aged person for having the limitations of not being able to adapt—rather than redesigning the structure to fit the age and capabilities of the population. That mindset needs to be disrupted.

Another area of our lives that the book suggests addressing is financial literacy. Not only are most people struggling to live day-to-day, very few are putting away money for retirement. Jenkins suggests that "What if, instead of saving for retirement, we think of it as saving for life?" Of course, the added idea in this category is the

55

encouragement to do our best to avoid spending beyond our means, and to get as debt-free as possible as quickly as possible. A key is both financial literacy and honest awareness of what really matters in a person's life. In my opinion, **rightsizing is the perfect solution.**

One of the most valuable suggestions I found in the book was the encouragement to "change the rules" that most of us have grown up believing in the area of aging. She suggests that we look at things like better transparency in healthcare, better management of Medicare costs and services, the need to reward caregivers, securing the solvency of social security, encouraging personal savings, promoting ongoing learning and education, and readapting our environment for an aging population.

While this book didn't cover everything I believe is important to positive aging in the days to come, it did raise many important questions. Most of us who are approaching an age when we can retire tend to forget that in terms of human lifespan it really hasn't been around very long. That means we must all design how we will play out our lives in the years to come. If life itself is an ongoing path of learning, growing and experiencing, maybe retirement as we often think of it needs to be rethought in a more positive, contributing and life-enhancing way.

Perhaps the SMART approach is to always remember that change will happen regardless of whether we like or dislike things just as they are. Recognizing that as truth, then we might as well join the conversation about the disruption of aging in order to experience it in the best possible way.

Chapter 7

Is "Purpose" The Magic Elixir For A Long, Happy & Healthy Life?

Oh, the worst of all tragedies is not to die young, but to live until I am seventy-five and yet not ever truly to have lived. ~ *Martin Luther King Jr.*

Open any magazine aimed at women over 30 and you are sure to see advertisements promoting the latest in anti-aging. Then as the years go by, it is nearly impossible to avoid the constant barrage of commercials claiming to have the secret to avoid ever getting old. Yet, if we pause for a moment before spending our hard-earned money, we know that the only real way to prevent aging is for our lives to end. Face it. The longer we live, the older we will get. Perhaps instead of fussing about how we look, or thinking we can live forever, what we truly want and crave is something that makes each day of that journey rich and meaningful. Fortunately, such an elixir is available to us all and doesn't cost a dime. That magic potion is to find and live a purposeful life.

Last summer my husband Thom and I heard author and purpose-cheerleader Richard J. Leider speak at a conference. As the founder of **Inventure—The Purpose Company**, Leider shares a convincing story of how and why purpose is so essential to all people, everywhere, regardless of their age. Leider believes that isolation and loneliness are rampant in our society and that, "If we aren't careful, we can begin to mistake our busyness for meaning—turning our lives into a checklist of to-dos that can occupy all the waking hours of our days..." His work also shows him that many people today are feeling unfulfilled and living in an "existential vacuum." The solution to all three issues—living a purposeful life.

Back in 2009, Leider participated in an extensive study done by the **Met Life Market Research Institute (MMI)**. The primary conclusion of the research revealed that people 25-74 feel that "meaning" was the most important factor to "living a good life." Of course, what defines a good life and what defines meaning varies from person to person. Still, at its core, the MMI Study showed that "regardless of age, gender, financial status or life phase, the majority of people assign the most importance to meaning-related activities and, above all else, spending time with friends and family." The conclusion: Meaning is age-proof, recession proof, and necessary to achieve the good life.

However, although purpose and meaning are important at all ages, it becomes even more so as people age. In addition, Leider is convinced that when people face a life-threatening illness or challenge, a clear purpose makes all the difference as to how satisfied and happy they believe themselves to be.

Unfortunately, four myths exist that often stand in the way of people thinking that purpose is necessary. Those myths are:

Myth #1: My purpose must be completely original. Many of us harbor the belief that a purpose must be grand and unique to be worthwhile. Instead, Leider assures us that most of the time we borrow, combine or modify our ideas to move forward with anything—purpose included. Our purpose is far more about deciding and then taking action, rather than coming up with something different or grand.

Myth #2: Only special, rich, educated or healthy people have a true purpose. Wrong! As Leider says, "one of the great truths about purpose is that it is not limited by circumstances. In fact, major challenges may offer the choice of new directions and purpose that can add years to a healthy life." Every single one of us has a purpose; we just have to do what we feel called to do.

Myth #3: Purpose must arrive by inspiration or revelation. Wrong again. Purpose can be anything that *we feel* gives our life meaning, no matter how trivial or uninteresting to others. Leider defines living on purpose as, "whenever we use our gifts and talents to respond to something we believe in, something larger than ourselves."

Myth #4: Purpose is a luxury and making a living takes priority. False! As author and philosopher, Viktor Frankl said, "Ever more people today have the means to live, but no meaning to live for." Sure, an opulent lifestyle might look good from the outside, but any life focused on just making money or getting by is wasting the precious resources we all hold inside.

According to Leider, the good news is that we all have a purpose within us. He believes that "unlocking your life purpose" is actually a process of self-awareness and choice and says, "purpose is played out every day in our choice points." Leider found his own purpose by following his own "fortuitous encounters." Eventually, he used his background in counseling and psychology training to begin writing, coaching and to start what he calls, "inventure" expeditions. By helping others unlock their purpose, he found his own.

But what about the rest of us? How do we discover and unlock our purpose? Leider offers three simple, but not necessarily easy, solutions:

- **Get clear on your life story.** Or as a recent blog post asked, "What is the point of your story?" The clearer we are on our life story, the more we recognize what is important to us and where our focus lies. Don't like your current focus? Change it. Then look around to see what life is asking of you.

- **Recognize your gifts.** We all have gifts and natural talents, but we must first acknowledge that they are ours and that we can use them. Leider suggests that we take the time to recognize our "most-enjoyed gifts" and then decide how to best give them away to something in which we genuinely believe in.

- **Unleash your curiosity.** Leider claims that "research points to curiosity as one of the key ingredients in longevity." He also believes that curiosity is an inner fire that leads to passion, and our passions are a clear path to our purpose.

Many other ideas and techniques exist on both Richard Leider's website or within his books. One of his very best ideas is that if you aren't clear about your purpose, you can always use Leider's default purpose. That "default" purpose is—to GROW and GIVE! If you wake up each day vowing to grow in some way and commit to giving it to others, your own individual purpose is sure to develop and deepen over time.

Other suggestions include filling in the blank to the question, "The reason I get up in the morning is to _____". How we answer leads to a purposeful mindset. Unfortunately, Leider says that one-third of us aren't clear about that question. Leider also recommends practicing mindfulness and spending time in self- reflection and meditation. After all, if we don't take the time to pause throughout our days and life, we will merely get caught up in a rat-race type existence.

During the last 30 years, Richard Leider asked thousands of people the question, "If you could live your life over again, what would you do differently?" It boiled down to three things:

- **I would be more reflective.** Again, people would do well to take the time to look carefully at their lives before they are in the midst of a crisis. When people know what is most important to them they can then take action to include more in their lives.

- **I would live with more courage.** While many said they would take more risks, what most meant is that they would risk being their true self and living more authentically. They also felt they would risk more in relationships, in work and in life itself, and stop worrying so much about "security."

- **I wish I had found, or lived, my purpose.**

Obviously, Leider is a passionate believer in the power of a purposeful life. Bottom line? He is convinced that the key to living longer, healthier and happier is for us to find our purpose and then share it with the world. Maybe instead of focusing on anti-aging or trying to look younger than we are, it would be very SMART to drink the magic elixir that living a life of purpose offers us all.

Chapter 8

9 Reasons Why What You Think About Aging Matters

Know that you are the perfect age. Each year is special and precious, for you shall only live it once. Be comfortable with growing older. ~Louise Hay

Henry Ford supposedly said, "If you think you can't—you can't. If you think you can—you can." While that statement usually applies to reaching our goals or persevering in spite of the odds, we seldom consider it in context with aging. Yet, growing research shows that our view of aging sometimes has a dramatic effect on the quality of our health, happiness, and wellbeing. Not only does what we each think about aging matter, how we feel about aging as a society influences the experience that each of us will have as the years add up. Fortunately, if we can learn to identify those stereotypical prejudices most of us hold about aging, we can halt and maybe even reverse many of the negatives formerly believed to be our destiny.

I'll bet there isn't a person alive in our country that hasn't heard a good joke lately about a senior citizen. Facebook is full of funny photos and captions showing older people as buffoons. Just about every situation comedy on television portrays elders in a negative light. No wonder none of us ever want to grow old! Is it possible we do ourselves a tremendous disservice every time we pass those cartoons around or laugh along with others when another senior is the butt of a joke?

That's what Becca Levy, an associate professor of psychology at the Yale School of Public Health and lead author of a current study on aging, believes. She is convinced that such negative stereotyping is a "public health issue." Ultimately it is possible that such a constant cultural mindset perpetuates an age-based stereotype threat (ABST), along with a prejudice and discrimination that are nearly as insidious as those surrounding racism or gender inequality.

The good news is that during the last 20 years a growing number of studies clearly demonstrate that what we think about and how we feel about aging changes the outcome of our lives. Nine of the most interesting are:

- A positive view of aging gives a person a 44% more likely chance to fully recover from a severe disability!

- *Believing* that aging offers opportunities for continued growth, rather than a decline or social loss, results in better subjective health, higher income, less loneliness, and greater hope.
- When trained in positive age stereotypes over the course of several weeks, participants began feeling more positive about their own aging self-image and then that, in turn, resulted in significantly improved physical functioning. Even more interesting is that when the training and messages were offered subliminally, rather than explicitly, the outcomes improved nearly 30%.
- Those subjected to negative aging stereotypes drive faster and much less safely.
- Negative aging stereotypes encourages poor and shakier handwriting.
- Being exposed to negative stereotypes about aging triggers added stress-heightened cardiovascular responses in the body, whether a person is aware of it or not.
- People who feel good about aging tend to take better care of themselves, practice preventative medicine, and eat better.
- Memory and brain function increased in older participants when subjected to positive aging subliminal messages that directly related to one's self-image. On the other hand, negative aging

subliminal messages resulted in poorer memory and brain function.

- Holding a positive view of aging gives a person an added 7.5 years of life over those with less positive views of aging! _

The good news is, as Professor Becca Levy says, "What people aren't aware of is that they have the ability to overcome and resist negative stereotypes" and "compensate for the ill effects of automatic ageism." Now that we know about some of the results of current studies, here are six things we can do to reverse some of the trends of negative aging stereotypes and feel better about ourselves as we age:

1. **Recognize the many benefits of aging.** Continue to educate yourself about the realities of aging—rather than blindly accepting the cultural bias. Selectively read information that increases your knowledge about the positive aspects of aging, while refusing to read or study those that imply otherwise.
2. **Exercise!** Studies show that people (especially women) feel better about their age when they exercise regularly.
3. **Stop watching so much television—especially comedies.** A study done in 2005 shows that the more a person watches television the more likely

they are to have a negative view of aging. Situation comedies are the worst. Also of concern is the invisibility of older adults and seniors on network programming in ways that contributes to the negative stereotyping of an aged population.

4. **Refuse to blame some of your experiences on your age.** Multitasking or not paying attention is usually the culprit behind memory problems, but many of us routinely blame it on our age. Stop it! In addition, many health issues like lack of flexibility, weight, and even poor health happen more as a response to our day-to-day life choices rather than our age. By recognizing the true cause of some of our experiences, we start realizing that age doesn't have to be as negative as we've sometimes believed.

5. **Hang around with people who see aging in a positive way and avoid those who don't.** Just like so many things in life, the people around us have a huge influence on our thinking and quality of life. While it might not be easy to break off from those who see aging in a negative way, our health and happiness actually depends upon it.

6. **Make a habit of thinking of the advantages of your advancing age rather than the detriments.** While thinking of ourselves as younger than we really are might be advantageous at times, as we age it is wise to stay open to the

opportunities of continuous growth and possibility. Even when there are certain things we can no longer do like we did when we were young, if we continue to develop new habits and ways to relate to the world and hold a positive perspective on that, the future can be hopeful.

We live in exciting times because the overall view of aging and what it means to all of us as we grow older is more positive than ever. Finding out why some people age in a positive and healthier way compared to others is under study by dozens of organizations on a regular basis. Learning to make the most of every stage of our lives is always SMART. And just like at all ages, staying aware of what we think and feel about others and ourselves is a key to a healthy and happy life.

Chapter 9

Why Happy Marriages & Relationships Are Key To Healthy & Positive Aging

Relish love in our old age! Aged love is like aged wine; it becomes more satisfying, more refreshing, more valuable, more appreciated and more intoxicating. ~Leo Buscaglia

Early this year Thom and I decided to experiment with our diet. We attended a lecture that warned us about how eating wheat and sugar was detrimental to a healthy and aging brain. That caught our attention. So during the next month we avoided bread, pasta or anything containing wheat. We also eliminated desserts, juice or any beverage with added sugars. While it wasn't without challenges, it wasn't that difficult either—mostly because we were doing it together. As the days go by, it's SMART to remember that some of the greatest gifts of long and happy relationships are the collective health, happiness, and well-being they offer.

I wasn't surprised to discover that research backs this up. People who are happy and report high life satisfaction tend to be healthier. Numerous studies support these facts showing that happy people have a stronger immune system, better heart function, are more resilient against stress, and even have a longer life *regardless* of their baseline fitness, differences in demographics, and even life circumstances. **Happier people are healthier people.**

Hand-in-hand is research that proves that those people in long-term relationships, either marriage or cohabitation, are positively influenced in the areas of life satisfaction and wellbeing. This is especially pronounced when the couple considers their partner to be their best friend. A study completed in 2015 by the "National Bureau of Economic Research" reports, "Those whose spouse or partner is also considered their best friend get almost twice as much additional life satisfaction from marriage or cohabitation as do others."

Of course, what isn't emphasized in many of these studies is that people who survive an unhappy relationship and divorce are likely much happier by themselves. I've always believed that being single is far better than being married to the wrong person. And let's not forget, as author Wayne Dyer said at one time, "If you are unhappy living in a particular town, chances are that moving to another town won't change that." On the flipside, if you are happy in one town you'll probably be equally happy in the next. Wherever you go, and with whom you are with, there you are.

But beyond the abundance of studies that reveal that happier people are healthier, married or not, a new study announced in 2016 took the information deeper. William J. Chopik from Michigan State University and Ed O'Brien from University of Chicago wanted to know *if just living with a happy person* could also affect a person's health in a positive way. They realized from previous research that "social contagion" plays a big part in a person's well-being, so they wanted to see if something similar occurred with a person's health. (In other words, like a contagion, we indirectly "infect" the people around us by our moods, beliefs, and actions either positively or negatively.) What this new study wanted to discover is whether, *"self-health is independently* predicted by the happiness of one's spouse."

Also important to notice, they deliberately studied over 22,000 married adults from age 50 to 94. Not only were they curious about how health might be affected as people age, great interest exists from the government and other groups to identify factors that may benefit and enhance health in our aging population. This study confirms that happier people are healthier people and at the same time offered evidence that happier partners lead to better self-health—even though the partner makes no conscious effort on their own. They proved it in five significant ways:

- The happiness level of our partners influences both our individual health and our behavior. As the study states, "…participants with *happy partners* were significantly more likely to report better health, experience less physical impairment, and exercise more frequently than participants with unhappy partners, even after accounting for the impact of their own happiness and other life circumstances. Again, none of these effects meaningfully diminished over time suggesting that having a happy partner could afford surprisingly long-lasting effects on a person's own health."

- The happiness level of one partner influences the other *regardless* of that person's own initial happiness. And, as the study states, "In most cases, the effects of the partner happiness on an individual's health increase over time."

- Other people, and most especially our romantic partner, influence us by their very presence. This impacts our own feelings, behaviors and the outcomes of our lives.

- Gender did not seem to change the results. In other words, regardless of whether you are a wife, a husband or any other type of partner, the results stayed true. Also relevant was, "The meaningful benefits of partner happiness are likely cumulative in nature and emerge only after significant time spent together;"

- No "self" lives in isolation. Those around us influence us on many levels. As the study explains, "...the self lives in rich social contexts comprised of other people who likely influence this process, perhaps no more so than a romantic partner. The current study demonstrates that happy partners seem to substitute as proxies for a happy self. Precisely because happiness is thought to fuel energy, happy spouses may devote more effort to improving the lives of their unhappy counterparts, who may be less motivated to do so on their own."

- The report goes on to explain how a happy romantic partner may likely influence the health of the other partner beyond that partner's own involvement. They speculate it happens in three ways:

- If one needs assistance, a happier partner is more likely to provide caretaking. Unhappy partners, not so much.

- A happy partner is more likely to help sync up healthier behaviors within the relationship with things like better sleep routines, better food choices, etc.

- A happier partner makes life easier, which leads to greater satisfaction and wellbeing in the other partner (regardless of that partner's own happiness set-point) so that they are more likely to avoid self-destructive behaviors like binge drinking or drug abuse.

As most of us know, emotional and behavioral contagion (see definition above) is **a well-known fact**. In other words, the people we hang out with on a regular basis have a subtle (and sometimes not so subtle) influence on our moods and our actions. This study goes further by confirming that the people around us, especially our romantic and long-term partners, can add or detract from our good health. This has far-reaching implications as we age.

So how did Thom's and my diet experiment work out? While neither of us saw a radical change in our health (we started out healthy so that didn't change) we did feel it was a positive direction in our lives. Cutting back on sugar, processed foods, breads, and pastas is surely a positive move for everyone. And like I said, doing it together with my best friend made it both relatively easy and even enjoyable.

Celebrating a holiday like Valentine's Day is often a way to show the connection between two people who are just beginning to realize how love can influence their happiness. Perhaps it would be SMART for all of us to realize that those we are closely connected with are influenced mentally, emotionally and physically by not only our love, but our level of happiness. Simply put, instead of giving flowers or candy this year, maybe our feelings of well-being and joy are the greatest gifts we can offer those we love.

Chapter 10

How Is Your Hearing? 5 Reasons It Matters!

The belief that youth is the happiest time of life is founded on a fallacy. The happiest person is the person who thinks the most interesting thoughts and we grow happier as we grow older. ~William Lyon Phelps

During the last several years I knew that my hearing wasn't as sharp as it used to be. But like millions of other baby boomers I told myself I was far too young to worry about it. But because I prefer preventative medicine to reactionary medicine, I decided to get a hearing test just to check things out. Even then I was somewhat shocked and dismayed to learn just how bad my hearing really was. After digging around on the Internet I was equally shocked to find out how common impaired hearing is for millions of Americans. Even more important is why the denial of it can become such a huge problem if left untreated.

According to a study in the Archives of Internal Medicine, up to 20% of Americans over the age of 12 have trouble hearing in one or both ears. That's one out of every five of us. Statistics also show that of those of us *willing to admit* we have a hearing loss, over 19% are ages 45 to 64 and nearly 30% are ages 65 to 74. Once you reach age 75, over 44% have hearing loss. And even though men are more likely to report hearing loss and blacks seem to do better than caucasians, nearly half of us will have to deal with it at some point in our lives.   Perhaps more baffling is that of all the people who are *willing to admit* to having a hearing problem, **only one in seven uses a hearing aid**.

What's The Problem?

The big problem is denial. For several reasons most of us don't want to admit that we can't hear like we used to think we could. Then, like me, even if we admit we might have a bit of a problem, we deny that it is bad enough to warrant taking action. There are several big clues that indicate whether any one of us really should take action. Here are five questions to ask yourself:

1. Do I believe some people talk too quietly or mumble a lot to be heard well?

2. Do I dislike talking on the telephone because the connection isn't clear or is sometimes difficult to hear?

3. Is it hard for me to follow the conversation in certain television shows (like *Downton Abbey)* because of the accents or diction even when I turn it up loud?

4. More than once a day do I ask my spouse/friends/children to speak up or repeat themselves?

5. Do I avoid talking to people in crowded noisy places especially if they are sitting or standing a couple of seats away from me?

If you answered yes to more than one of these questions you probably have a problem that you've been denying. And remember, even when people are willing to admit that they might have a bit of a hearing problem, only one in seven is willing to take the steps to correct it. What is even more tragic is that people with what is considered to be severe hearing loss were just about as likely to deny they had a problem as those with mild or moderate loss.

What Are The Reasons For Denial?

As might be expected there are lots of studies being done to try to determine causes for hearing loss and what people are doing, or not doing, about it. The most common causes for hearing impairment are genetics, exposure to extremely loud noises, certain illnesses and/or their corresponding treatments, and even head injuries. Who among us hasn't wondered about the price of listening to loud music? **Research shows** there are five top reasons people don't take steps to treat hearing loss.

1. **Finances.** Hearing aids are expensive. I got my first case of sticker shock when I went to Costco and learned from the technician that the recommended Costco Brand costs $1,800. Just like with most people, hearing aids are not covered by my insurance making it cost prohibitive for many people.

2. **Stigma.** Let's face it. Most of us tend to believe only old people wear hearing aids even though my research proves otherwise. And while I don't believe myself to be overly concerned with the aging process and my own mortality, it does beg the question in a big way.

3. **Hassle.** Most of us are busy people and being instructed to maintain and care for an expensive item that we never before had to think about can be daunting.

4. **Lack of knowledge or bad experience.** Many people are unsure of how to proceed and others were given faulty advice in the past leading to a bad experience.

5. **Attitude** about hearing aids. Most of us have heard negative reviews from people who wore hearing aids, leading us to believe they often don't help at all. Some of this is certainly valid but most has to do with lack of education.

Why Correcting Impaired Hearing Really Matters

I must confess I was in no initial hurry to rush out and buy the expensive hearing aids that were recommended to me. Even though I know and trust the technician at Costco where I had my hearing test, I still wanted to believe it wasn't that bad. All the excuses I listed above were running through my head. That was until I began researching this article and learned the five big reasons addressing impaired hearing really matters:

1. **Hearing loss can lead to cognitive decline and to all types of dementia.** While questions remain whether wearing a hearing aid can actually reverse this trend, there is no doubt there is a correlation. Simply put--not hearing changes our brains in a negative way.

2. **Hearing loss causes problems with memory.** Diminished hearing stresses our cognitive load which makes memory increasingly challenged.

3. **Hearing loss affects our brain structure and shrinks our gray matter.** Anything that isn't used, shrinks and atrophies. Again, our brain processing is being altered by not being able to hear.

4. **Hearing loss leads to a growing social isolation that contributes to dozens of health related issues.**

5. **Hearing loss leads to poor balance, increased falls and slower movement as people age.**

Until I was willing to face the facts of my own hearing loss I remained blindly unaware of how prevalent the issue is for so many of us. Sure, most of us would prefer that we all stayed fully functioning and fit for our entire lives, but that seldom happens, especially if we reach the advanced ages we seek. And no one wants to spend money if they don't have to. But denial seldom improves anything. Instead, maybe it's SMART to remind ourselves that how well we hear without aids does not define who we are or our self worth. But, how well our brain hears and processes does help us to wholly experience life and to connect to others. As someone who intends to live life as fully as possible and as long as possible, why would I not take action to make it as good as possible? Why wouldn't any of us do the same?

*Reference to the individual studies quoted in this article are available through links found on SMARTLiving365.com.

Chapter 11

What Makes A Life Go Well?

Do not grow old, no matter how long you live. Never cease to stand like curious children before the great mystery into which we were born. ~Albert Einstein

As many of you know, a recurring question on my blog SMART Living 365 is, "how can we live a happy, healthy and meaningful life?" Another way of saying that is, "What makes a life go well?" I recently came across the work of a man named Dr. Nick Baylis who has spent his career in pursuit of that question. Baylis, a "wellbeing" consultant and psychologist, teaches at Cambridge University in the UK where he helped to co-found The Well-Being Institute. He is also the author of several books and is known as Dr. Feel Good in his column written for ***The Times*** (London). One of the first to lecture on the field of positive psychology in the UK, Baylis is convinced that the "science" of wellbeing is a practice of identifying and then utilizing the skills that lead to a life well-lived.

Just what does an all-around life of wellbeing mean? According to Baylis, he believes that this state is achieved "by the skill and the will to create something beautiful out of whatever life throws our way, whether setback or successes, tragedies or triumphs and to do so in harmony with a healthy Natural World." He is equally convinced that our culture and educational system are geared toward increasing isolation and passive consumerism (TV, computers, iphones, etc.). Unfortunately, those activities usually keep us from other actions that often lead to the greatest elements of a satisfied life like: creating close personal relationships (for life, sport, creative community activities and problem solving projects.)

Contrary to what advertising usually pushes, those things that bring the greatest pleasure are often much more deliberate and simple. Things like slowing down and relaxing, savoring what we already have, investing in ourselves whole-heartedly, keeping life and the world around us as clear/close/hands-on as possible—all aspects that work together to make our life feel more rewarding.

In an effort to identify many of the skills demonstrated by those whose lives are happy, healthy, helpful and good-hearted, Baylis wrote his first book entitled, **Wonderful Lives**. But the lives of the people he writes about are not perfect; instead as he says, "A wonderful life doesn't mean a life that's trouble free or without fault. It means it's wonderful that the person is still smiling and going strong after all they've been through." In his book Baylis features 50 inspiring people who he classifies as living a wonderful life. Out of those examples, Baylis then identifies four major life skills he believes helped to create these lives of wellbeing. They are:

1. **Partnering-Up with Good People.**
   According to Baylis, the breadth and depth of our personal relationships are crucial to our wellbeing. Baylis continually recites example after example of people who, in spite of the odds, achieved a rewarding life as long as they found at least one person to love and encourage them. In fact, Baylis believes, "When someone loves us, it helps us learn to love and care for ourselves."

2. **Becoming an Expert In our Favorite Pursuits.** Baylis believes it is a mistake to think that people are either born with a particular talent or not. He is convinced that no matter what our age, we have the ability to learn and become good at anything we are passionate about. The lives of the people he studied proved that anyone who was willing

91

to practice repeatedly at something they loved, and had the guidance and support of those who could help them nurture that passion, nearly always went on to live a wonderful life.

3. **Helping Mind and Body to Thrive and Flourish.** There should be no surprise that Baylis uncovered that one of the keys to wellbeing is a healthy mind and body. His work stresses the importance of adequate sleep, diet, nutrition and physical activity. But he also emphasizes that true health includes a mind that is curious, peaceful, self-motivated, and self-disciplined. While we tend to think of negative habits when it comes to what we should or shouldn't eat or drink, Baylis believes that the mental negative habits that we continue to entertain are equally destructive. Balance and moderation in ones' lifestyle usually leads to greater wellbeing.

4. **Choosing and Changing our Journey's and Life Directions.** The people that Baylis interviewed that created a life of true wellbeing learned to follow their own heart-felt values and top priorities over the course

of their lives. Rather than trying to please others, those with wonderful lives managed to stay true to themselves and change courses when necessary. They also didn't give up and managed to bounce back and be resilient when things didn't work out the way they planned. They put their passions above the pursuit of money or material success, and as Baylis says, "put themselves in the right size pond."

As usual, most of these keys to wellbeing aren't new. Those of us who've been reading or studying them during the last ten years have heard them all one way or another. What I particularly liked about the approach by Dr. Nick Baylis was the continual reminder that, "It's not that there is a right way to live, or some sure-fire formula for success; it's just that some particular approaches, skills and experiences do undoubtedly increase the likelihood of things working out rather well." And even if we've heard them before, hearing them over and over again is a way to reinforce their effectiveness.

Another thing I appreciate about Baylis is his approach to aging. He is convinced that our minds and our bodies are "wonderfully plastic" and will continue to grow and adapt far into our maturity. He says, "...life tends to get better the more skills we acquire for living it and age has little bearing on this equation. It seems nature doesn't intend that old age is the price we pay for living. Aging is not a disease, nor does it bring inevitable decline. It's an opportunity--extra time to make a positive difference and explore our relationship with life more deeply so the familiar can be seen through fresh eyes."

Finally, it's possible that the best idea offered by Dr. Baylis is his suggestion that we approach the pursuit of wellbeing or happiness not as a destination we hope to arrive at, but a skill that we continually practice and apply to our lives in the best ways we can. Seeing wellbeing as a skill answers our human need to continually be reaching forward and make progress in a way that is authentic, playful and optimistic. And although Baylis believes that happiness can't be taught. "…it can be learned…by a bold, hands-on, exploration and experimentation, and an adventurous curiosity for what helps a life go well."

In the end it seems that, like so many things on the path, it is SMART to remember we are the only one that can truly make our life go well.

Chapter 12

Growing Whole Instead Of Old

Every year should teach you something valuable;
whether you get the lesson is up to you. Every year brings
you closer to expressing your whole and healed self.
~Oprah Winfrey

Since turning 60 I've been increasingly interested in
what it means to grow older in a vibrant and purposeful
way. Much like my work with rightsizing, I see aging not
as an inevitable loss or sacrifice, but instead as an
opportunity to get to the heart of what really matters to
each of us as living, breathing beings on this planet—and
then sharing that with our community and the world. Plus,
with so many of us nearing retirement age, and yet living
many years after, isn't it SMART to recognize that making
the most of those years seldom happens by chance? So
instead of merely growing old and waiting for the
unavoidable, learning what makes us whole and happy is
worthy of our attention.

What do I mean by growing whole? For most of us, I think becoming whole can be narrowed down to four elements.

- Finding and sharing our purpose;

- Being self-aware, conscious and mindful;

- Recognizing our connection to others and the planet as living beings;

- Connecting and balancing our body, mind and spirit.

A man who consistently teaches others to find and share their purpose is Richard J. Leider. Last year I read the book **Life Reimagined** that Leider coauthored and found it inspiring and useful. Even better was attending a lecture that Leider gave at a conference that Thom and I attended in 2016.

Leider is convinced that even though we all want to have fun and enjoy our leisure as we age, having purpose is far more important. In fact, he boldly says, "Without that purpose, you grow old." The good news is that he offers us a "default" purpose that most of us will likely feel comfortable using. That default is "growing and giving." If every single morning we each woke up and asked ourselves, "how will I grow today and what will I give?" that question can provide us with unlimited purpose for the rest of our lives. Then almost automatically as we explore "growing and giving," we likely will find unique and exciting ways to bring our purpose into the world.

When you approach aging with the intention of sharing your purpose, becoming self-aware and more conscious is almost required. Again, this approach fits hand-in-hand with rightsizing on an internal level by urging us to become more conscious of our own motivations, what we have learned in our lives, what is important to us, and why we believe we matter. The more mindful and aware we are, the more we will learn to love and accept ourselves. We also feel freer to share that with the world.

On the flip side, without awareness, we can grow bored and tired of just cramming our days full of leisure activities. An audio talk I listened to this morning about retirement said that many people when they first retire are convinced that retirement means they can finally just think about themselves for once in their lives. In other words, many have spent the majority of their life doing things they felt obligated to do and now retired, they feel free to let all that go. But is it ever that easy to fully let go of obligation and guilt if you've lived your life that way? And perhaps an even better question is, why not replace that guilt and obligation with the gift of your true Self for the rest of your life? That will benefit you, and everyone else as well.

Next, I think that recognizing our connection to others and the world is a critical element of becoming whole. When you think about it, is it even possible to be whole when you consider yourself a separate and distinct individual without connection? Plus, it is becoming increasingly apparent through study after scientific study that isolation is extremely detrimental to our health. I think the latest I've read is that deep connections can add up to seven years to your life. So regardless of whether you want to extend your connection to all of life on the planet and what that means on a cosmic level, just growing and enhancing close personal relationships with a circle of friends will help to keep you alive and happy as you age.

Last but not least, I think the road to wholeness requires us to balance our health, our mind, and our spirit into one being. That union means that we are a complete system, not just made up of individual and separate parts. While some of us like to think we are spiritual beings dragging a body around, there are equally as many who believe our body/mind is primary and any "spirit" is just a chemical reaction in our brain. I tend to believe we are all of it. As whole beings, we are body, mind, and spirit infinitely connected to everything else.

For even greater clarification, recognizing what is not whole is also valuable. Here are a few things I think makes for a divided or fractured life:

- Never taking the time to discover your passions, needs or place in the world.

- Following the advice of everyone else and never listening to your inner voice.

- Denying parts of you that don't look attractive or "nice."

- Thinking that it doesn't really matter what you do because it won't affect anyone else.

- Letting fear rule your life and refusing to interact with others.

- Believing that you are an island and don't need others.

- Thinking of yourself in only one small dimensional way without acknowledging your past, present and future.

- Spending your days so busy that you never have time to think about what really matters.

- Working only on staying young and healthy while feeding your mind nothing but gossip, television and junk food for the brain.

- Going numb to what is happening in your body, with your friends, or your world. Or, as Richard Leider says, we succumb to "...inner kill—the condition of dying without knowing it."

No matter what our age, we all want to believe we matter. Becoming whole answers that need on every level. Having a purpose, staying aware and mindful, recognizing our connection to others and balancing our body, mind and soul all lead to a sense of wholeness. From there, instead of fearing the prospect of growing older, the SMART thing to do is to put our focus on growing more whole. Then no matter what occurs, we will be able to experience the best in ourselves and offer that to others as long as we can draw a breath.

Chapter 13

Volunteering—Seven Reasons Why Serving Others Serves Us

With age comes the inner, the higher life. Who would be forever young, to dwell always in externals? ~Elizabeth Cady Stanton

For four years I volunteered for a local organization called **The Ophelia Project** where I mentored teenage girls enrolled in high school. Not well known, I first learned of the organization from another volunteer named Sandy who told me how much she loved the experience. She explained that although it was an eight-month long commitment per year, adding up to about 12-15 hours a month, the time spent was some of the most rewarding things she did in her life. Right after that conversation, I got in touch with the director of Ophelia and signed up.

Sandy was right—it was a big commitment and quite a bit of work. But she was also right about the benefits. Looking back over my life I must admit that most of my happiest times have occurred when I was actively engaged in helping others. That's why it should come as no surprise that it is practically impossible to create a happy, meaningful and rewarding life without being of service to others in some small way. Even more, new information about philanthropy shows that serving others ultimately serves us in many ways. Here are the top seven benefits we each gain by compassionate helping.

1. **More happiness.** According to Stephen G. Post, professor of preventative medicine at Stony Brook University in New York and author of ***The Hidden Gifts of Helping***, a part of our brain lights up when we help others. That part of our brain then doles out feel-good chemicals like dopamine, and possibly serotonin. According to Post, "These chemicals help us feel joy and delight—helper's high." A common reaction is that "some people feel more tranquil, peaceful, serene; others, warmer and more trusting." When we volunteer we often give ourselves deeper purpose and meaning and that nearly always leads to greater happiness.

2. **Reduce stress.** When we help others our bodies release a hormone called oxytocin, which buffers stress and helps us maintain

social trust and tranquility. Along with oxytocin are the other chemicals like dopamine, which is a mood-elevating neurotransmitter. These drugs tend to push aside negative emotions and reduce the stress level.

3. **Relief from pain.** A study done by *Pain Management Nursing* reports that on a scale from 0 to 10 that people's pain ratings dropped from nearly 6 to below 4 after attending a volunteer training program and leading discussion groups for fellow sufferers. Volunteering takes our mind off our pain and also makes us feel more in control of the experience.

4. **Longer lifespan.** Over 40 international studies confirm that volunteering can add years to your life. In fact, current studies suggest up to a 22% reduction in mortality rates! How much do we have to do? Studies confirm that a regular commitment of as little as 25 hours per year is beneficial.

5. **Lower blood pressure.** A study done by *Psychology & Aging* reports those adults over 50 who volunteered for 200 hours in the

past year were 40% less likely to have hypertension than non-volunteers. It is believed this is accomplished because of the lower stress, and the effects of being active, social and altruistic.

6. **Reduce mild depression.** A study of alcoholics going through AA (Alcoholics Anonymous) points out that those who volunteered to help others were twice as likely to stay clean a year later and their depression rates were correspondingly lower as well. Plus, in many cases mild depression is linked to isolation. Volunteering helps to keep a person in regular contact with others and to help develop a social support system.

7. **Benefit your career.** That's right. A book entitled *The Halo Effect* by John Raynolds insists that volunteering for the right reasons can so turn your life around that the benefits will extend to your work. Raynolds says, "Remember, when you become involved, when you lead with your heart as well as your head, the result is always good." Instead of feeling depressed or unfulfilled at work, Raynolds is convinced that you will feel more happy, confident and energized when you

find something that makes you feel generous and purposeful—and that of course will spread to every single area of your life.

So does all volunteering prove beneficial? No. Stephanie Brown, Ph.D. associate professor of preventative medicine at Stony Brook University in New York says, "You have to genuinely care." In other words, feeling resentment or obligation will erase the benefits that we might otherwise receive in both our emotions and our physiology. If you feel exploited in any way it is better not to take the action than stress yourself out doing something for the wrong reason.

My time as a volunteer isn't always fun—there is usually time, energy and even money involved—but it is always meaningful and gratifying. Looking back at the times when I helped at a local food distribution service, delivered gifts for seniors, helped a young boy get braces, wrote a check when I could, and so much more, my feelings of contributing to others and my community have always boosted my awareness of the blessings in my life.

A central theme to all my writing is discussing ideas that can lead to a happy, peaceful and meaningful life for each of us. Even though there are lots of ways to do that, and some of them seem incredibly obvious, if you're any thing like me you appreciate being reminded of ideas that often slip under the radar or are routinely taken for granted. Volunteering and serving others are like that. So even if you already know that volunteering offers huge benefits, but haven't done it in a while, it's definitely SMART to make it a regular part of your life.

Chapter 14

Is Cohousing A Good Solution To Aging Well?

Count your age by friends, not years. Count your life by smiles, not tears. ~John Lennon

Cohousing isn't a new concept. In fact, humans have been coming together in community for thousands of years to survive and thrive. What is new is that these days many of us have grown so independent and disconnected that we've forgotten why community is important in the first place. Maybe when we are young, busy, and focused on the needs of one's immediate family, that isn't so important. But eventually, if people begin to value experiences, relationships, and good health more than the stuff they accumulate and the accolades they obtain as they age, things start changing. That's when being a part of a strong and vibrant community starts sounding more and more appealing. It's also when the idea of cohousing may pop up as a solution. Is it a key to helping people age better? Those who have embraced it say, "Yes!"

During a 2016 conference titled, **"Cohousing: Aging Better Together"**, architect Charles (Chuck) Durrett admitted that with cohousing, "We aren't doing anything that hasn't been done before, but now we are doing it consciously." He and his wife Kathryn (Katie) McCamant coined the word "cohousing" and pioneered the movement here in the United States after visiting Denmark in the 1980s. The design and overwhelming benefits of the lifestyle so intrigued them that together they have gone on to help create over 50 cohousing communities here in the U.S.

According to Durrett, the key to cohousing is the design. Unlike the traditional "consumer model of housing" where a person shops around trying to find a home and a good neighborhood, cohousing takes a more proactive approach by putting the neighborhood and community first. And how do you do that? As Durrett says, "It's cohousing math. 1 + 1 = 3." In other words, when people come together consciously to design a neighborhood the way they would really like it to be, what they end up creating is a community that fits their needs in multiple ways. The camaraderie, the memories, the shared decisions, all add up to shared history and connection. As Durrett said, "Proximity is an ally to the process and effort is connected to happiness."

While most existing cohousing communities are multi-generational (meaning they allow children and all age groups), the new trend appears to be senior cohousing. As Eric Cress from Urban Development Partners (UDP) said about the vertical model of cohousing his company is building in Portland, OR, "This generation of seniors is not going to conform to prior aging models." Cress is excited about the possibilities of cohousing and continued with, "This is the time for developers like us to influence how people age in a vibrant way.

What every speaker at the conference seemed to agree on was that cohousing brings people together. And when people come together, they thrive—especially as they age. Is it challenging to live so closely and interdependently as the cohousing model? Yes, it can be. But as one person said, "Yesterday I was playing bridge, today I'm creating a neighborhood." Not only do cohousing communities work together to create a neighborhood that satisfies them all on a deep level, but the very act of working together in proximity adds to their connections. As Durrett says, "Cooperation is really the windfall and ultimately trumps the architecture." The creation of a cohousing community allows each member to get in touch with what is most important to them, what they really want in a home and a neighborhood. That, in turn, gets them in touch with what they want to "be" in the future. That valuable awareness is important no matter what a person's age, but it is particularly important as a senior.

A big part of the design in every cohousing community is the Common House. While each home is typically individual and private, a large common house with communal facilities like a commercial-grade kitchen and meeting rooms is critical. The reason the Common House is so important is because people need to "run into each other and break bread together." Another element in the design is making walkways and front doors visible to each other so that it is easy to connect. For that reason, garages and parking are usually on the periphery of the property. Why? Because, as Durrett says, "My relationship with my neighbor is more important than my relationship to my car." What else goes into the typical cohousing community? While it really depends on the people who helped design and create it, a community garden, green and sustainable features, barbecue areas, workshops, and art rooms seem to be part of most.

What makes them different than a condo or any senior housing community like a **Del Webb Sun City**? While similarities certainly exist, a cohousing community is self-created, self-managed and self-maintained. Sure, it's always possible to hire someone to do that work, but it is in the learning to work together and create that some of the most powerful connections develop. People also discover what is most important to them, what they are willing to pay for and maintain, and to actively participate in their life and community on an ongoing basis.

How do you start a cohousing community? Fortunately, Durrett and McCamant have authored a book entitled, *Creating Cohousing * Building Sustainable Communities* along with a series of related books on the subject that details how to get started. Also, the **"Cohousing Association of the United States,"** **(Coho/US)** maintains a website with pages of information listing existing communities, how to form a new community, and hundreds of articles about the process. Plus it is always possible to visit many of the existing cohousing communities around the country and get a feel for the people and the lifestyle before committing.

If any downside exists it appears to be with affordability. The process of developing and building a new community is both pricey and laborious due to current building costs, and both city and state building codes. As one young mother said when talking about her cohousing community in Fort Collins, Colorado, "I bought here years ago and love it. But I wouldn't be able to afford it now. I don't know how any young family could."

While cohousing may not be for everyone, there is no denying that bringing people together in community is healthy for all of us. As more and more of us discover that relationships and experiences are far more rewarding than big Mac-Mansions in the suburbs, and as the media continues to report that loneliness and disconnection can cut nearly ten years off of a person's lifetime, discovering new ways to create a community deserves our attention.

A large number of us, baby boomers included, are demanding a better way to live out the remainder of our lives. Instead of merely sitting back and letting our lives unfold by default, cohousing is one way to be SMART and create a future lifestyle "by design." As Alice Alexander, Executive Director of Coho/US and a resident of a cohousing community said about her decision to live there, "It's even better than you think."

Chapter 15

Baby Boomers, Marijuana, And Aging Well

The great thing about getting older is that you become more mellow. Things aren't as black and white, and you become much more tolerant. You can see the good in things much more easily rather than getting enraged as you used to do when you were young. ~Maeve Binchy

Like most baby boomers who grew up in California and nearly half of the U.S. population, I tried marijuana as a teenager. The few times my girlfriends and I managed to get our hands on a joint, we would light it, pass it around and then spend several harmless hours giggling and acting silly. But once we matured, like most other adults I knew, we moved on to the far more legal and acceptable form of getting high—alcohol. And although some opportunities to give pot another try presented itself in the four decades since then, public aversion to smoking, the illegality, and the stigma, made it preferable to avoid. Now, things are changing—dramatically. Not only has California voted to make recreational pot legal, our aging population is discovering the numerous medicinal benefits it offers to many who want to age as well as possible. Maybe it's time for another look.

How Fast Are Things Changing?

In 2000, according to surveys done by Gallup, only about 30% of the U.S. population favored making marijuana legal. Fast forward to October of 2015 and Gallup now reports that 58% of the population supports recreational legalization. And while younger generations have always been more open to experimenting with substances, baby boomers are quickly shifting in that direction as they age. On the medical front, The Harris Poll reports that as of May 2015, four out of five adults (81%) favor medicinal legalization, up from 74% in just four years.

What's Driving The Change?

While no definite proof exists, it is clear that aging baby boomers who vote are a key. While they may have grown up with warnings that pot was a dangerous and illegal drug, most boomers didn't experience it that way. However, as they raised their children throughout the 70s, 80s, and 90s, they often acted on the side of safety and kept it out of the house. But that was then. Now at an older and hopefully wiser age, most baby boomers admit that pot is likely no more dangerous than alcohol. And to be honest, it is far less dangerous (not to mention less expensive) than many medications prescribed by doctors.

In fact, research now shows that pot is less risky than many other drugs even though it is still considered a Schedule One Controlled Substance by our government. That puts cannabis in the same category as heroin, LSD, and cocaine. But a study by the British Government in 2010 shows otherwise by documenting how alcohol is more dangerous than 20 legal and illegal substances. Employing 16 measures of "harm," which included damage to health, potential for dependency, economic costs and detriment to society, alcohol came in at the highest score of 72. Heroin scored at 55, while crack cocaine rated a 54. Even tobacco garnered a higher rating of 26, versus marijuana at 20.

With media attention now highlighting the problems with other drugs and food, pot seems less problematic. Another study done by Gallup in June of 2016 showed that nearly half of our population believes prescription painkillers are far more harmful than cigarettes, alcohol or marijuana.

Plus, addiction rehab facilities report that more than one-half of all admissions are due to alcohol, and alcohol mixed with secondary drugs like prescription painkillers, antidepressants, and tranquilizers. Of course, baby boomers are all too familiar with motivations for such medication. Many women over 50 know that complications from menopause, normal aches, and pains of aging, balancing dependent children and aged parents, trouble sleeping, and normal life stresses make it helpful to have alternatives.

Is Pot The Solution?

Like many things, the benefits of marijuana depend on the individual and every person's unique needs. What is becoming increasingly apparent are the possible health advantages available through its use. Although research has been stymied here in the U.S. because of antiquated drug laws, several countries around the globe like Israel, Canada, and the Netherlands continue to fund research into the indisputable benefits of cannabis. Also, a small but courageous group of physicians here in the U.S. have fought the odds and managed to make progress on a growing list of medical uses. In fact, a **survey by** Webmd.com reports that 56% of all doctors in the U.S. agreed that marijuana should be legal for medical purposes nationwide.

Some of the most promising **benefits of medicinal marijuana** are:

- Nausea Relief—particularly in relation to chemo for cancer or AIDS patients.
- Nerve pain—particularly related to diabetes, spinal cord injuries, AIDS, and others.
- MS (Multiple Sclerosis)—controlling spasms, stiffness and helping with sleep.
- Chronic Pain Relief—mixed results in effectiveness for different conditions.
- Crohn's Disease and other intestinal disorders—eases the need for medication or surgery related to inflammatory bowel disease.
- Cancer treatment—shown to slow or halt the growth of certain cancer tumors. A recent study into treating breast cancer is also underway.
- Parkinson's Disease—helps with tremors and pain.
- Alzheimer's Disease—so far tests are inconclusive about helping to slow down or prevent, but more studies are necessary.
- Anxiety Disorders—reduces stress and anxiety in certain situations.
- PTSD (Post-Traumatic Stress Disorder)—Mixed results to date for reducing nightmares and worsening symptoms. More tests are necessary.

- Epileptic seizures—very useful for controlling seizures in both children and adults.
- Glaucoma—temporary decrease in intraocular pressure.
- Sleep disorders—relaxing the body and mind for a better night's sleep.

Even with the shortage of research being done, one of the more exciting discoveries is that when isolated, a particular cannabinoid has been identified (called CBD) that does not make people "high" when administered. This non-psychotropic compound seems to counteract the cognitive impairment of cannabis and is particularly beneficial for promoting sleep, relieving convulsion, inflammation, anxiety, and nausea. As more and more states approve legalization, the research and potential of this medicinal plant will continue to unfold.

But Why Make Recreational Pot Legal?

With growing evidence that cannabis can help people as they age or deal with illness, is there any reason to continue keeping it as an illegal drug? Some people say yes. With so little research, some doctors believe that we don't yet know enough about what it can do and what complications might arise. Dosage and potency can also be uncertain.

But the argument for legalization is growing increasingly powerful. After all, if ongoing studies show that alcohol and tobacco use is even more problematic, then why is the government standing in the way of personal choice for individuals over 21?

Of course, money might turn out to be the biggest game-changer. Most Americans, even those who are not in favor of using it themselves, recognize the enormous amount of tax revenues generated in states where it is legal. Just like with the sale of alcohol and tobacco, taxing individuals who choose to partake significantly enhances the state coffers for a variety of public needs.

Another significant financial benefit in states with legalized pot comes from the reduction in policing, prosecuting and then holding in prison millions of citizens for marijuana possession. According to a study done by the ACLU in 2013, every 37 seconds a person is arrested for possession, costing the United States $3.6 billion (yes billion!) to prosecute in one year (2010) alone.

In addition, recent research by Health Affairs determined that in states where patients had access to medical marijuana, medical costs for drug use dropped dramatically. In 2013 alone, Medicare saved $165 million in states that gave people the option of using marijuana instead of prescription meds. Estimates say that it would save Medicare $470 million if all states allowed the choice. And that doesn't even address the advantage of getting many people off dangerous and addictive prescription medications. It also ignores the fact that a study shows that there are nearly 25% fewer deaths caused by accidental overdose when pot is available medicinally.

Of course, two of the biggest groups in opposition to legalization are privately owned prisons as well as drug companies. Those two organizations realize that making pot legal will change their bottom lines and they have every reason to fight legalization.

Are There Dangers?

After spending three days researching the benefits and problems of wider usage of marijuana, I found four areas of concern. As most would likely imagine, the biggest problem is with children and teenagers having greater access. Studies have shown that regular use by young people affects the healthy development of the brain, including a permanent loss of I.Q. For that reason, specific care and ongoing public education should be enacted to guard against such occurrences. But as with alcohol or cigarettes, safeguarding children should be an ongoing pursuit.

Another area of concern shows that those who may be susceptible to schizophrenia are vulnerable to marijuana use triggering the condition. Although likely a genetic link, anyone with a family history of that disorder should be cautious.

Finally, one of the most challenging things about the rapidly expanding pot industry is standardization and dosing guidelines. Although edibles eliminate the need for anyone to smoke to receive benefits, it appears that dosage and potency are variable. Because edibles take longer to metabolize in the human body, and size and weight is a factor, it is very easy to overdo treatment, especially when covered with chocolate! Unlike alcohol or even smoking, eating anything infused with cannabis is best done with patience, education and restraint especially when starting out.

What about addiction? Existing studies indicate that the addiction rate when marijuana is widely available will level out at approximately 9% for those consistently using it. While this certainly needs to be watched and treatment offered, it is lower than the addiction rate of alcohol at 15%, and cigarettes at a whopping 32%.

The SMART Approach

The point of this chapter is not to convince anyone that marijuana should, or shouldn't, be a part of your life. But even if you'd agree that some things like too much alcohol, sugar, red meat and hours sitting in front of the TV are not good for you—few of us want the government telling us as adults when, or even if, we can make our own choices. Perhaps even more at issue is whether our government should be allowed to continue to block research that may prove to be enormously valuable for millions of Americans.

Keep in mind that every single thing we consume, and every action we take, carries consequences. Marijuana is no different. With that known, it is always SMART for each of us to do our own research, consider the findings, and recognize our individual unique needs before making a responsible choice. And then, like with most things, moderation is usually the SMART path to take.

*Reference to the individual studies quoted in this article are available through links found on SMARTLiving365.com.

Chapter 16

Awakening Your Super Genes For A Happy, Healthy & Long Life

Of all the self-fulfilling prophecies in our culture the assumption that aging means decline and poor health is probably the deadliest. ~ *Marilyn Ferguson*

Many of us believe that our genes are similar to a cosmic lottery. Some get lucky and are born with healthy and strong genes—others not so much. If we are fortunate enough to have parents who've lived a vibrant and healthy life into their nineties we feel blessed. The rest of us usually cringe when our doctor asks us at our annual checkup, "Who in your family experienced this, this and that?" —often dreadful diseases that we never want to experience. But is it luck or something else?

A new book with cutting-edge research challenges that old assumption. *Super Genes—Unlock the Astonishing Power of Your DNA for Optimum Health and Well-Being* written by Deepak Chopra, M.D. and

Rudolph Tanzi, Ph.D. claims that the new study of genetics shows us, "...in the vast majority of cases regarding health and personality, your genetic destiny is not set in stone."

First some background. As some of us know, during the last two decades the Human Genome Project completed a map of the 3 billion chemical base pairs of genes that make up the double helix of DNA in every cell of our bodies. According to Chopra and Tanzi, this genome, or super genome, that we all possess is made up of three big components:

1. The approximately 23,000 genes you inherited from your parents, along with 97% of the DNA located between those genes.
2. The epigenetic switching mechanisms that reside in every strand of DNA, which is controlled by your epigenome.
3. Genes contained in the approximately 100 trillion microbes (comprising between 500 and 2,000 species of bacteria) in our bodies that continually serve us.

What most of us probably don't know is that all those building blocks within us are "...fluid, dynamic and responsive to everything you think and do." In fact, the major premise of this book is that "...gene activity is largely under our control." By learning how our genes operate, and what influences are possible, we can "make our genes help us" and activate an enormous amount of untapped potential for a healthier life—hence, "super genes."

So how does all this work? Keep in mind that DNA is the brain of each of our cells. According to Chopra and Tanzi, 99.9% of the time they work wonderfully. Only in the tiniest .1% is there trouble. Within our DNA, only 3% of it is made up of genes, but those genes direct and trigger certain actions for each cell. It's important to realize, "…there is no such thing as a 'disease gene.' All genes are 'good' and provide a normal function needed by the body. It's the variants that they harbor that can bring problems."

Some variants determine our height or hair color. Others determine whether we have a predisposition to a disease. But remember, Chopra and Tanzi assert that, "The bottom line is that what we do, what we experience, and how we view the world, along with what we are exposed to in our environment, strongly influence the actual outcome of the genes we inherit."

A key to understanding how we can learn to influence our genes is found within the study of epigenetics. Epigenetics are the managers or control switches that either trigger on or off the variants and/or mutations in our genes. This collection of epigenetics, called an epigenome, constantly monitors our daily lives. For example, "...a growing body of evidence indicates that diet, behavior, stress levels and chemical pollutants can all affect gene activity and thus one's survival and well-being."

What are some of the most provocative claims reported in the book? Here are important ones that caught my eye:

- "What makes the difference between well-being and radical well-being is learning to guide and influence your genes in a positive manner."

- "After studying hundreds of pairs of identical twins, researchers determined that the probability for Alzheimer's disease occurring in both twins is 79% if one of them is afflicted. This means that lifestyle accounts for 21% of the probability of developing Alzheimer's *even with identical genes*."

- "For various cancers—colon, prostate, breast, and lung—the heritability in identical twins ranges from 25% to 40%, which is why the current view holds that the majority of cancers, perhaps a large majority, are preventable."

- Studies have shown that up to one-third of dementia cases are linked to mineral deficiencies or poor diet.

- The food we eat, our level of stress, our lack of exercise and so much more causes negative epigenetic modifications and alters gene activities.

- Only about 5% of disease mutations guarantee that a particular kind of disease will begin within any of us. The other 95% only *increase our susceptibility*, along with the environment and other choices in a person's lifestyle.

- "When it comes to human disease, whether it's cancer, diabetes, heart disease or Alzheimer's, to name a few, inflammation is almost always the killer that takes the patient out. If you want to name the epigenetic change that plays the biggest role in modulating a biological process, it would probably be inflammation."

- "Drastic inactivity (sitting all day with no exercise at all) eventually leads to a 30% higher mortality rate for men and double the mortality rate for women."

- "Lack of sleep has been associated with triggering Alzheimer's…"

But make no mistake, this book isn't just about cutting-edge gene study facts. Entire chapters are devoted to which foods are most beneficial, proven ways to reduce stress, valuable ways to exercise and even how important our thoughts and attitudes are for creating super genes. They also show that, like so much in the study of happiness and positive psychology, super genes respond to the outlook and beliefs we hold in our mind. Having an **optimistic growth mindset** once again shows that regardless of the genes we have been dealt in life, there are ways we can positively influence them to our benefit.

Chopra and Tanzi repeatedly remind us that our genes are not the enemy, but instead are often only responding to the "cloud of causes" that our every day choices and thoughts bring into existence. They make it clear that our biology is *never* our unalterable destiny. Ultimately this book reminds us that it is SMART to insure that our actions, choices, habits, and thoughts work in harmony with our bodies and our world in order to experience an ongoing healthy and happy life.

Chapter 17

New Evidence That Planning and Goal Setting Are Keys To Positive Aging

None are so old as those who have outlived enthusiasm. ~Henry David Thoreau

Like most people my age I am increasingly interested in what leads to aging well and happy. I am also keenly aware of how different that is from many of the conversations my parents had in later years. Rather than go through a depressing list of "organ – recitals" that often characterized our parents and their friends, the new emerging conversation about positive aging is leading in exciting and interesting directions every day. One recent study from the Netherlands combines the idea of healthy aging to people's hopes, plans and wishes for their future. Could it be that having goals and planning for certain experiences can make us happier and more satisfied as we age? This particular study says yes.

In the past, most studies about aging were conducted from an objective approach to the topic. That perspective on aging usually put a person's physical functioning and health status above all else. Former studies also put heavy emphasis on financial security, physical appearance and sense of purpose. So even though the world we live in is dramatically different in 2017, previous studies mostly offered information on the physical and material nature of aging.

Fortunately, groups of researchers are now approaching the subject in new and more personal perspectives. These new studies ask participants what is important to them and what their experiences are as they age. These innovative, more multidimensional approaches incorporate a person's physical functioning, quality of health, well-being, life satisfaction, engagement, social life, and the ability to adapt into the results. For those of us most interested, a new understanding of what leads to positive aging is unfolding.

Using Research To Show The Benefits Of Planning For The Future

One such study was led by Dr. Johanna M. Huijg from the Leyden Academy on Vitality and Ageing in the Netherlands. She and her colleagues decided to take on something that many people already suspect—that it is beneficial to always have something to look forward to as we age. In 2016 Huijg and her team started by asking a group of older individuals about their future plans and wishes, as well as what they would like to achieve in life. By taking this approach they resolved a quandary found in previous research. That problem was that when older individuals were asked, approximately 50% felt they were "aging successfully." Yet, based upon the former objective measures of successful aging, only 10 to 18% qualified. Clearly how many researchers saw aging, and how people felt about their own aging process, looked different depending on who is doing the looking.

This new study about plans and wishes asked 649 individuals from age 55 to 90 a variety of questions about their future. At the core of the study were questions about individual desires and hopes for the future. Beyond that they asked people to rate the quality of their health, whether they were working or not, and whether they did volunteer work.

Researchers also paid particular attention to whether participants had poor social contacts or were completely happy with the number and closeness of their relationships. In addition, each person was asked to rate their life satisfaction and their optimism about the future. Study authors then tied these elements together to reveal interesting information about whether or not planning offered people a good way to age in a positive way.

What Did They Discover About Positive Aging?

The most interesting results of this study revealed that people who admitted to having plans and goals in at least two areas of their life experienced higher life satisfaction than all the rest In other words, it is important for us all to have something to reach for in the future. Those participants who reported no goals or plans, or those who had very low wishes for the future, rated much lower on the life-satisfaction scale. It also showed that while health was an important goal, it wasn't the primary goal as previous research had made it out to be.

Of all the plans and wishes that people had, the majority emphasized activities. Over 50% of those listed involved plans to stay active in life, pursue hobbies, and to engage in ongoing learning and intellectual activities. But, no surprise here, the overall goal activity was traveling. Nearly 38% said they wanted to see the world.

Following activities of all sorts was the desire to stay engaged with life. This meant that participants wanted to continue with productive activity, work, and interpersonal relationships. Next, people wanted to stay healthy, overcome an illness, or reach a certain age. Overall, the majority of people had a combination of goals and plans for the future with the top three being: activities, engagement in life, and good health.

After that came the desire to be happy and enjoy life. Next was a goal to stay mobile, live independently, and have financial security. Lastly came the desire for the health and wellbeing of others and world peace. Again, these results show how much of previous research misses the mark when it comes to what is most important to people. Although marketing concerns tend to focus on an obsession with making sure that we all have enough in savings and that we plan for retirement, this study suggests that those thoughts don't consume our dreams and goals as much as they would like.

The study went further by making correlations between certain categories of information. The study reports: "There was a significant relationship between lower education and not having PWs (plans and wishes) as well as for a considerable lack of social contacts and not having PWs." In other words, those with low education and few friends often had little or no goals or plans for what lies ahead.

In addition, while health did take a role in some people's goals and plans for the future, it was usually in a secondary position. That is likely because health helps in the pursuit of all other plans and goals no matter what people are hoping to experience. It also confirmed the importance of a person's ability to adapt and change as they age. Having a willingness to be flexible and to continue to set and reach goals appropriate to one's life situation lies at the center of a person's desire to keep planning and setting goals no matter what.

For those of us who like to plan, and especially plan to age well and happy, this research is encouraging. But keep in mind, how we plan and wish for the future looks different to many of us. I recently spoke to a friend who said she wasn't a good planner. Yet I've witnessed her execute a plan to create a beautiful piece of artwork that staggered my mind. So planning doesn't always look like a to-do list. Sometimes planning is just holding a strong desire to see or create something new in our future—be it artwork, a book, learning a language or traveling the world.

I am reminded of a memory of my mother years ago when I asked her why she didn't quit smoking after experiencing several health problems. As encouragement I asked her, "Don't you want to live to be 80 or 90?" She answered in all seriousness, "Why would I want to do that?" Maybe that's why I find this new research so exciting. Sure it confirms that good health and strong social connections are important. But perhaps more essential is the continuous ability to hold dreams in mind and make plans for the future. It appears that maintaining a positive attitude about the future, and expecting that our good will continue to unfold in ways that we plan for, just might be the SMART thing to do for those of us who want to age in a successful and positive way.

*Reference to the individual studies quoted in this article are available through links found on SMARTLiving365.com.

Chapter 18

Do You Know The Point Of Your Life Story?

*My physical body may be less efficient and less
beautiful in old age. But God has given me an enormous
compensation: my mind is richer my Soul is broader and
my wisdom is at a peak. I am so happy with the riches of my
advanced peak age that, contrary to Faust, I would not wish
to return to youth.* ~Robert Muller

Last night Thom and I sat down to watch a new **Syfy**
thriller on television. Although the reviews were
promising, after about a half hour of watching things blow
up, people dying, and young-twenty-somethings behave in
idiotic ways, we turned it off. After all, what was the point?
That question has been on my mind after finishing a book
entitled **The Point Is** by Lee Eisenberg. The author
believes that how we answer that question should help
each of us make sense of birth, death and everything in
between. And maybe, just maybe, answering it on a
regular basis could assist us in living SMART and making
the most of every precious moment of our lives.

Unfortunately, a lot of what seems to happen is that many people's lives appear to ramble along without a consistent or meaningful point. And yes, I can be guilty of that myself now and then. Whenever we rush around, filling up our days with busy work or habitual activities, whenever we live unconsciously doing things we think other people want, whenever we take the easy way out because it doesn't seem to matter, we are muddling up the point. *Our* point. Then like the television program from last night, perhaps it's time just to turn it off?

Naturally, a journalist and author like Eisenberg believes the key to finding out the point of our lives is for us each to create a story out of it all. Whatever narrative we use for our ever-evolving story allows us to, "link our 'reconstructed past' –how we remember things, accurately or not—with our imagined future." To the extent we hone our narrating skills and create a story that gradually becomes complete, coherent and ultimately meaningful, to that degree do the "points" of our lives become fulfilling and satisfying.

Yet Eisenberg doesn't just let it all go with that statement. Instead, like any writer, he weaves together elements of his learning and understanding to showcase how every story evolves. Of course, there is the beginning, middle and ending which all must add up to something significant to both the storyteller and anyone else who is listening.

Do the themes and events in our story matter? Yes and no. What matters most in any story is **what we choose to remember** and where it goes from there. The author quotes Gerald M. Edelman, a Nobel Prize winner with, "Every act of perception is to some degree an act of creation, and every act of memory is to some degree an act of imagination."

Eisenberg is also a fan of thinking through the prologue to our life stories. Don't believe you have one? Were you born a blank slate or were you pre-loaded with some form of software? Were you born into bliss or born into sin? What is the legacy of your species? What prejudices does your culture hold? What does all that mean to you as an individual? While we seldom take the time to think about it, it matters to our story. Eisenberg says, "How you conjure your prestory can have a definite bearing on what you expect the ultimate point of your life to be."

Once we get going with our narrative it is common to focus on the turning points that stand out in our memories. Those key, or "nuclear episodes" help to move the story forward in a predictable way. Those wisdom events are usually a time when we undergo a significant change in our lives. Discovering your calling in high school, meeting your soul mate, confronting the person who betrayed you, landing that coveted job, getting cancer, writing that book, are all pivotal points that can all lead up to the point behind it all.

But as any writer knows, it's the middle of the story that can get bogged down and cause trouble. Why? Because if a writer (or a person living their life) waits until the middle to start wondering about the point of it all and how it might end, then the entire story can often stall or go completely off the rails. Whether it's a life, an article, or a book, it's the same. If I start a blog post without knowing what my point is, I'll find myself in the middle with a bunch of words on a page and confused about what comes next. So, why should a midlife crisis be a surprise when people find themselves nearing 50 with no idea how they got there and fear about what comes next.

Eisenberg believes a key to avoiding a pointless life is to get past a hazy passivity, idle uselessness, and disengagement with life. Instead, he says, "A meaningful life is one that satisfies desires; connects to something beyond yourself; and results in something of objective, positive value." But going even further, it is collectively weaving the memories and events in our lives and recognizing that we are moving onward and upward in a progressively positive way. Ultimately, "It's the shape of a life that matters."

The challenge, of course, is not to let the final stage, or third part of the story, end up in a downward-sloping slog. Now that so many of us are living for extended years in "biological sterility," the larger point of our lives has nothing to do with all of us in the process.

Of course, all writers struggle with wondering when the story is complete. Every post I write I am tempted to add another paragraph, to clarify something else more fully, to explore a new idea. But when is enough, enough? Similarly, is there ever a right time to die? By first overcoming the strangeness of death and any fears and aversions we hold, it's beneficial to wrap up our narratives on a high, rather than a painful descent into fear, pain and suffering. As Eisenberg says, "The main thing is that a story, long or short, and a life story, long or short, be well resolved by the end. Does the story deliver? And does it satisfy?"

There are a lot of other writing tips in the book and lots of questions about how we view life and death. But best of all is Eisenberg's admonition, "The point is to write the best story we can. The point is to keep the story from obsessing over what's lacking, inferior, or ugly in life and instead cast our attention on the good, the true, and the beautiful, never overlooking the pain or injustice but confronting them." While those elements might not be the point of your personal story, it might be SMART to include them in at least one of your chapters.

Chapter 19

Studies Prove Your Mindset Determines How You Age

When it comes to staying young, a mind-lift beats a face-lift any day. ~Marty Buccella

Do your thoughts determine how you age? The answer is "Yes" according to Professor Ellen Langer. During the last forty-five years, this Harvard social psychologist has studied the way our mindset affects both our health and how we age. At the core of her work is unifying the mind and the body rather than how the conventional medical and psychological world typically treats each as separate. Langer is convinced that a unity offers a far better understanding and hope for making positive change. Fortunately, her studies provide us with plenty of science to back up her assertions.

For those who may not have read last week's blog post, Ellen Langer teaches in the Psychology Department at Harvard University and is the first woman ever tenured there. She is the author of eleven published books and over 200 articles. Of all her work, the one titled *Counterclockwise* is the most influential and gets to the heart of her ideas about the mind/body connection.

Counterclockwise asks the question: Can you remember who you were and how you felt 20 years ago? And if yes, how might that influence your body and mind today? With those questions in mind, Langer and her students recruited two groups of older senior men in their late 70s to early 80s. Back in 1979, this was when 80 really meant 80—so these guys were truly old. None of these men lived alone making them dependent on either a family member or a nursing home facility. Many walked with a cane and all needed a support system for the majority of their needs.

Before the study began each man was carefully tested for what was considered to be biomarkers for age at that time—everything from memory and cognition, to flexibility, dexterity, grip strength, and of course their hearing and vision. Even their mental state was recorded.

Then Langer divided the 16 men into two groups and at separate times took them to a retreat center that had been carefully replicated to look exactly as it would have 20 years earlier—1959. Everything in the retreat center was meticulously designed to ensure that nothing in the house appeared older than 1959; the black and white television in the living area, the appliances in the kitchen, and the magazines on the coffee tables. All records in the record player came from 1959 or earlier, and all the TV programs and movies came from that earlier period. Mirrors were removed and only clothing of the era was allowed.

Each man was told in advance that they would be part of a study, but not that the study had anything to do with aging. It was explained to the second group that their mission was to reminisce about the past. In contrast, the primary group was instructed to *act as if* it was actually 1959 in every way. They were encouraged to psychologically attempt to *be the person* they were 20 years earlier. They were also coached to only talk about events and happenings that had occurred in the world or to them, prior to 1959.

Also important was the fact that both groups were treated as though they were 20 years younger. They were required to carry their own luggage, help with dinner and cleanup, and make up their own rooms.

When the study concluded, they again tested all the men. Surprisingly, both groups of men (the control group and the primary group) registered noticeable improvement in some areas including hearing, vision, and memory. But, showing even more improvement were those in the primary group who also registered greater flexibility, faster gait, greater manual dexterity (where their fingers actually lengthened in spite of arthritis), and improved posture. Sixty-three percent of them scored higher on intelligence.

Also of note was the fact that although they had arrived extremely dependent upon either family or institutions to manage their needs, each man began functioning independently almost immediately upon arrival. Photos taken prior to the study and at the end, showing a visual difference. Independent observers rated the seniors, although still senior, as looking somewhat younger and more vibrant.

The results were so astounding that Langer hesitated to publish the outcome at the time, believing that she would not be taken seriously as a scientist if she did. However, ever since that time her research has continued to root out the numerous ways that our mindsets and thoughts influence our bodies.

The next study by Langer also confirmed the mind/body connection. Called the Chambermaid Study, this research shows that after hotel maids were educated to see how their daily actions could be perceived as healthy exercise—and with doing nothing different than just believing their work was indeed exercise—they lost weight, and their BMI and blood pressure improved. In other words, what people believe about their work and how they perceive exercise is connected to how their body responds.

Langer and her team then went on to study memory in a group of nursing home residents. First, everyone was given a memory test. Then ½ of the residents were asked to pay mindful attention to certain things in their home. To encourage that action they were offered incentives to recall certain things and events when asked. As Langer says, "Because they wanted the gifts, the information we asked them to track now mattered to them."

After a three-week period they found that *"when remembering mattered, memory improved."* But that wasn't the only benefit, those offered incentives and instructed to be more mindful also became more cognitively aware—they paid better attention to other people around them, their rooms, and the nurses—and even increased their longevity in the years following the study.

Langer also reminds us of other research that demonstrates how our use of certain words has the power to "prime" us. After reading words associated with being old and aged, looking at photos of older people or items associated with advanced age, or doing tasks that focus us on what our society thinks it means to be older, we can prime ourselves so that our bodies respond in a slower and more limited fashion. Everything from the speed of our movements, to our eyesight, memory, and cognitive awareness can be affected.

And what about time? In one study Langer showed that when people are fooled into believing they didn't get enough sleep, they did worse on memory tests. When they were fooled into believing they received more sleep than they actually did—they scored better. In addition, tests about blood glucose levels being affected by perceived time are also relevant. When subjects believed that time was faster than normal, their blood sugar spiked accordingly. When time was "slowed down," the blood sugar responded in kind.

These, and nearly all of the studies done by Langer and her students demonstrate that *if* you can effectively change the mindset or perception of a person, you can often influence some of the physical responses in the person as well. This applies to the health of the individual, as well as how they age. One of Langer's most well-known students, psychologist Beccy Levy, along with her colleagues claimed after a study, that "those who viewed aging more positively lived, on average, seven and a half years longer than those who were negative." Other research titled the Berlin Aging Study "found that dissatisfaction with aging was one of the principle factors in how long people live." Again, if we can adjust our mindset, we can influence our body in more ways than we normally realize.

Fortunately, as Langer asks, "if our beliefs have influence on our well-being, surely we can learn to influence our beliefs?" Of course, fundamental to that idea is that we must be willing to believe we have some control over our own health. How can we do that? Here are several things Langer believes is crucial:

- First, we must be mindful or aware of the world around us as much as possible. Langer recommends, "Pay attention to what is new."

- Notice differences and variables instead of loss or decrements. Just because something changes doesn't make it bad or wrong.

- Recognize that the world is designed by younger people with different capabilities— but rather than seeing lost capabilities as a physical problem—choose to see them as a design issue.

- Realize everything is contextual. Sometimes just changing the context opens up a world of possibility.

- Refuse to be merely a number or statistic. We are all unique and that includes what is happening to us on a physical level as well.

- Get second (or third) opinions on anything related to your health or important decisions—and then stay mindful and open about the answers.

- Refuse to be labeled—especially in a way that limits you or "primes" you to believe you can't do something.

- Counteract negative stereotypes for aging or health. Refuse to be boxed in. "Change the game."

- Stop associating pain or disability with age. Seek other explanations for what is happening and understand that issues can happen at most any age.

- Refuse to be "over-helped." Helplessness and dependence interferes with both our mental state and often our physical state as well.

As Langer says, "our attitudes, ideas, and beliefs are at least as important to health as our diets and our doctors." Yet many of us continue to believe the stereotypes of aging or related health conditions as ones of decline, decay, and inevitable loss. Langer goes on to say, "Our mindless decisions—our deference to doctors' opinions, our willingness to accept diagnoses, even the way we talk about our illnesses—can have drastic effects on our physical well-being." For those of us who want to age in a positive and healthy way, it is SMART to remember how much our mindset plays in the process.

Final Thoughts

Do not grow old, no matter how long you live. Never cease to stand like curious children before the great mystery into which we were born. ~*Albert Einstein*

Throughout this book I've done my best to remind us all that it is a privilege to age. Not everyone gets the chance. However, how we choose to age is something we individually get to design according to our attitude and beliefs. Will your future be a time of worry and fear about increasing decline and loss or instead, an ongoing period of adaptation and renewal? Will it be a time of regret and disappointment, or a time of optimism and hope? Will it be an ongoing adventure or a time of resigned distress? Regardless of our unique circumstances, the choice about how we intend to think about, plan for, and then respond, is really up to us.

Hopefully the research and stories I've shared have managed to elevate your thinking about what it means to age. We live in an exciting time to take advantage of all the upcoming technological, medical and psychological breakthroughs occurring just about every day around the subject. I also firmly believe that you and I, no matter what your age, will help change the perspective on aging to one of increasing possibility and fulfillment. Not only do we owe that to each other, but we owe that to the generations to follow. Perhaps even more important, we can use this information to strive for the best possible experience we are capable of as we live out the remainder of our lives.

Of course I do believe that we can use help and support along the way. Here are five reminders that I plan to keep reaching for in the days ahead:

1. **Learn to keep my mind trained to the positive about aging.** I personally use meditation and journaling to focus my mind on a regular basis, but there are numerous ways to get from where you are to where you want to be. Yoga or tai chi, certain types of exercise, mindfulness training or even hypnosis can help. Once we learn to direct our minds towards the thoughts we want in our lives....

2. **Stay focused on the positives and benefits of aging.** Sure there is information everywhere we look that implies the worst of it, but often that is because our minds are drawn to anything that threatens our survival. But as you grow more aware, you'll

find all sorts of positive things being reported. Need some more inspiration? Start reading my blog SMART Living 365.com on a regular basis. Besides that…

3. **Hang out with people that inspire you and talk positively about aging.** I am continually reminded that when I seek out inspiring people of advanced age that I am encouraged on a very deep level about aging. If I get together with people who only want to talk about what is going wrong with them (or the world) I immediately feel my world close in and helplessness take over. We do have a choice. And being as conscious about the people inhabiting our mental space is as much (or more) important as the food we eat or the exercise we do. Which leads to….

4. **Be conscious and willing to do what it takes to eat, sleep and take care of your body, mind and soul.** I realize this isn't easy. I personally have a couple of health challenges in my body that I never had to address when I was young. But rather than pretend that they will go away or turn my health (and my future) over to anyone else— including a doctor—denies the influence

that I can make by making changes as necessary. What works for me is to imagine that any health challenge I have is my body and soul telling me what needs to be adjusted for a longer and happy life. Of course, this requires us all to….

5. **Be adaptive and resilient.** I realize that some of us have an easier time with life than others. However, if we start knowing in our heart that we can not only survive any adversity that we face, but thrive as well, then happiness and wellbeing rest on the other side. This is where the other four reminders will come in handy as well. Training our brain to stay positive no matter what, keeping our minds focused and aware, hanging out with people who encourage our overcoming and inspire us, and doing whatever is in our power to stay healthy and happy are all important.

May the days ahead of you be filled with amazing possibility, inspired growth and increasing peace and wellbeing no matter what circumstances you meet along the way. I guess it is evident that I believe that each of us holds a large part of our future in our own hands. To illustrate that, I'll finish up here with one of my favorite stories.

Once upon a time some young boys tried to fool a wise old woman who lived in their village. The boys, who had seen the woman hobble about town just couldn't understand why the adults always seemed to treat her with respect. Putting their heads together, they schemed to find a way to show how pathetic she really was. Routinely they tried to come up with questions they thought she'd never be able to answer—but she always had something wise and relevant to say. Still, they never stopped trying to trip her up.

One day a particularly mischievous boy in the group came up with the perfect question that would be impossible for the old woman to answer correctly. He plotted to hold a small live bird behind his back in his cupped hands. He would then ask the wise woman, "Is the bird in my hands alive or is it dead?" Naturally, if the woman said the bird was alive, the boy intended to quickly squeeze the life out of it and answer, "No, the bird is dead." If the woman said the bird is dead, then the boy would merely present the live bird proving her wrong. Either way, the boy laughed thinking he couldn't lose.

One day soon, the crowd of boys found the old woman walking the streets of their village. The ringleader of the group had his live bird hidden away and when he spotted the woman, he stepped boldly in front of her, holding the small bird behind his back. "Wise woman," he challenged her with a smirk, "is the bird in my hands alive, or is it dead?

The woman was no stranger to these types of challenges or these types of boys. She paused patiently and looked around meeting the eyes of each of the boys before finally leaning over the boy in front of her and met him on eye level. Slowly, without fear, she said, "Young man, the life you are holding—is in your hands."

ABOUT THE AUTHOR

Kathy Gottberg has authored hundreds of newsletters, articles, blog posts and five books during the last thirty years. Her insatiable curiosity continually leads her imagination, along with her writing, in all sorts of diverse and interesting directions. That's why she has proudly authored four works of nonfiction and one novel. Her current passion is writing and blogging at SMART Living 365.com where she explores practical ideas and experiences that lead to happiness, peace and well-being for all. Also relevant to those paths are positive aging and retirement.

Kathy and her husband Thom have been partners in life and love for the last 40 years. They, and their dog Kloe, live in La Quinta, CA.

Current work and projects:

kathygottberg.com

smartliving365.com

Social Media Contacts:

Twitter: twitter.com/gottgreen

Facebook: www.facebook.com/SMARTLiving365

Pinterest: www.pinterest.com/gottgreen

Goodreads: www.goodreads.com/Kathygottberg

Made in the USA
San Bernardino, CA
25 January 2018